PERCEPTUAL TRAINING IN THE CURRICULUM

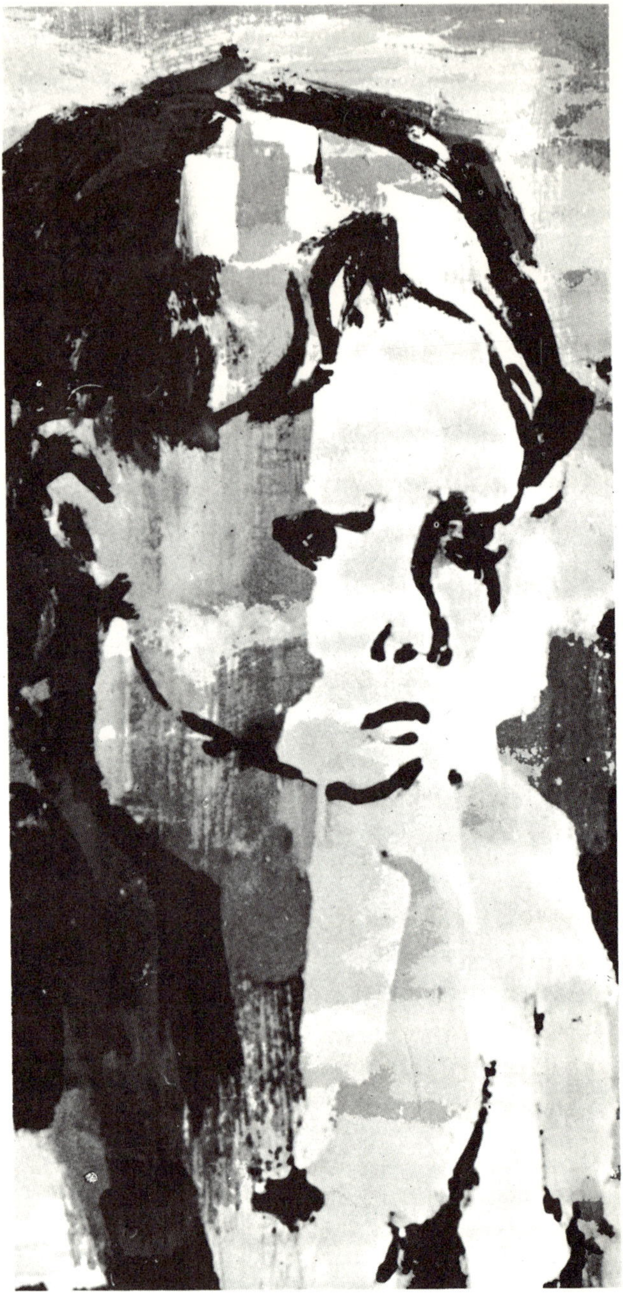

GEORGE H. EARLY
Achievement Center for Children
Purdue University

PERCEPTUAL TRAINING IN THE CURRICULUM

Illustrations by CAROL STERLING
Line Diagrams by LESTER DAVIS, JR.

CHARLES E. MERRILL PUBLISHING COMPANY
Columbus, Ohio   *A Bell & Howell Company*

© 1969 by Charles E. Merrill Publishing Company, Columbus, Ohio. All rights reserved. No part of this book may be reproduced in any form, by mimeograph or any other means, without permission in writing from the publisher.

Standard Book Number: 675-09537-9 (hardbound edition)
675-09536-0 (paperbound edition)
Library of Congress Catalog Card Number: 69-12182

1 2 3 4 5 6 7 8 9 10 — 73 72 71 70 69

Printed in the United States of America

THE SLOW LEARNER SERIES
edited by
NEWELL C. KEPHART, Ph.D.

For Peter

Editor's Introduction

The primary responsibility of the public schools is to teach — to develop in the child a body of skills, attitudes, and knowledge which will permit him to adjust to his environment and contribute to the society in which he lives. The slow learner presents a challenge to this basic educational task. Certain learning procedures and processes are disturbed in the slow learner so that the normal presentations by which teaching is customarily accomplished do not function, or function to a greatly reduced degree.

The difficulty lies in the child. His learning processes deviate from the normal either in kind or amount or both. Since learning is an all-embracing problem which transcends the specialized tasks of the school, the major concern should be directed toward therapeutic procedures which will reduce the learning problem and permit the child to learn from the great mass of experiences both in and out of the classroom. When research and clinical investigations began to reveal specialized therapeutic techniques which could ameliorate the learning disability, educators were naturally eager to provide such opportunities for the children under their care.

The result has been the development of a large number of excellent programs for the treatment of slow learners. The assumption is that, after remedial help, the child can learn from the typical classroom presentations or at least can profit from these presentations to a greater degree. Experience is beginning to indicate that, at least in many such cases, this assumption is correct.

In some programs, virtually all attention has come to be devoted to remedial techniques, and the teaching function of the school is delayed until remediation is complete. If the remediation period is extensive, as it frequently is, the child sometimes finds himself deprived of information which is offered to his peers. While therapy is occurring, he drops further and further behind in his general fund of information to the point where, when therapy is complete, he finds he has only exchanged one problem for another.

The amount of information required by the child in our modern civilization is staggering. From year to year as he grows, both the amount and the acceleration with which it must be assimilated increase. Any interruption in the process of assimilation throws him further behind. Exclusive attention to therapeutic activities, often rather remote from the stream of learning, represents such an interruption. We seem to say to the child in effect, "When you can learn like other children, then I will teach you what you need to know." Sometimes the resulting delay is costly.

The apparent dichotomy between therapy and teaching need not exist. The slow learner characteristically shows marked discrepancies in ability. In one area of performance the child may function very poorly. In other area, however, he may function very well. This fact suggests that probably in one or more areas he can be taught rather well and can absorb the informational data which he needs. Therefore teaching is possible through one set of learning functions at the same time that remediation is being attempted in less adequate areas.

Furthermore, informational presentations, by incorporating therapeutic techniques, can provide therapy as well as teaching. Strong areas can be used to bolster weak areas. Therapeutic activities can be directed so that they result in the discovery of information. Skills being taught therapeutically can be applied, as they develop, to the gathering of information. Thus, the teaching function and the therapeutic function can proceed side by side. Some of the most effective therapy has resulted from such a coordination of these two functions.

The present volume presents some examples of such coordination. Therapeutic procedures in the perceptual-motor area have been incorporated into classroom processes so that information is provided to the child along with activities to aid in the development of basic learning skills. At the same time, the teaching function has been made more flexible so that intact abilities in the child can bolster and encourage weaker functions. The whole is based upon units of study which can provide organized bodies of information. Thus, the demands both of therapy and of teaching are served.

Although the material presented represents only examples, it can be used to guide the teacher in the development of similar classroom procedures. Units of study prescribed by the curriculum can be altered to introduce perceptual-motor and other therapeutic procedures and can be liberalized to permit more efficient learning in the face of the child's handicap. In this way, the overall efficiency of the classroom activity, from the point of view of its basic objective, learning, can be increased.

N. C. KEPHART

Glen Haven Achievement Center
Fort Collins, Colorado

Contents

Editor's Introduction   ix

Chapter 1.   The Problem and an Approach   3

>
> *A Theory of Perceptual Development,* 6
> >*The Structured Self and the Structured World,* 7
> >*The Motor Basis of Internal Structure,* 10
> >*Developing the Motor Base,* 11
> >*Structuring Space,* 15
> >*Structuring Time,* 20
>
> *From Theory to Remediation,* 23
> >*The Curriculum as a Source of Perceptual Training,* 27

Chapter 2.   Perceptual Training with Social Studies   33

> *The Project: An Overview,* 35
> >*Construction Phase,* 39
> >*Use Phase,* 54
>
> *Conclusion,* 58

Chapter 3.   Perceptual Training with the Language Arts   61

> *The Unit: An Overview,* 62
> *Unit: Beginning Reading with Experience Charts,* 66

Chapter 4. Perceptual Training in a Science Unit   93

>   *Conceptual Background, 93*
>   *Conducting the Unit, 96*
>   *A Science Unit: Force, Energy, and Power, 98*

Chapter 5. Perceptual Training in an Industrial Arts Unit   149

>   *Conducting the Unit, 150*
>   *An Industrial Arts Unit: Small Gasoline Engines;*
>   *Disassembly, Assembly, Nomenclature, and*
>   *Functioning, 154*

Appendix. Constructing a Styrofoam Sphere   165

Bibliography   169

PERCEPTUAL TRAINING IN THE CURRICULUM

chapter 1

The Problem and an Approach

Teachers and other educators are showing increasing concern for children who have learning problems. Concern is warranted, and most welcome. A highly developed society is making increased demands upon its members. Those who cannot meet the demands, who cannot keep up, are finding that hardly any place exists for them in the bright, brave world which is mushrooming into being before our eyes. Generally speaking, children who do well in school will be able, as adults, to meet the demands of this complex world, but those who do poorly will not be able to keep up later. The school experience becomes an ever more important factor in equipping children for functioning in the world. Since school achievement is such a crucial matter, every method for helping the slow learner should be explored thoroughly.

Many children who do not achieve their full potential in school have perceptual problems. Such children do not see, hear, feel, and otherwise experience the world about them in the same way most people do. Perception involves both receiving information from the world and organizing that information into some meaningful pattern or form. If a child does not receive the correct information through his senses, or if he receives correct information but cannot organize it properly, perceptual difficulties occur and, quite understandably, he will have problems in school. Children with perceptual problems typically achieve below their potential in one or more academic areas. Further, their perceptual problems often make it difficult for teachers or other professionals to determine just what their potential might be.

Perceptual training can help many children who have perceptual handicaps. This training consists of remedial activities designed to correct a child's basic perceptual difficulties. Where a perceptual problem is interfering with learning, perceptual training deals with the root of the problem. Many schools are conducting perceptual training and, as information on the subject becomes more widely known, many others are planning similar efforts. Some schools have special classes exclusively for children with perceptual handicaps. Others conduct perceptual training as a regular part of their remedial programs in a variety of special-education classrooms. In still others, teachers have been using these training techniques with slow learners in regular classrooms. While as yet no single pattern for conducting perceptual training has emerged, awareness is rapidly growing that many children have perceptual deficits, that these deficits can result in lack of school achievement, and, most important of all, that something can be done to improve the situation.

Introducing perceptual training into a classroom confronts the teacher with a very large problem: How shall he conduct perceptual training with some children without neglecting the main task of teaching the regular academic subject matter to the whole class? In attending to the primary academic task, he finds that time for basic remedial work is often limited. On the other hand, if remedial procedures are attempted, the academic work may suffer. Many teachers have recognized the need for perceptual training, have discovered the rich resources available for such training, but have been discouraged by the conflicting demands of the academic and the remedial tasks.

This book presents an approach to the problem which should help resolve the dilemma. It suggests ways of using certain aspects of the academic curriculum itself as activities for perceptual training. This suggested approach involves teacher modifications of some curricular activities so that those activities result in perceptual training. If modifications can be made, then academic and perceptual training often can be combined, and perceptual training will not be an entirely isolated group of activities which compete with academic training.

The suggestion to modify some curricular activities does not in the least mean that all perceptual training should be done in this fashion. Perceptual training in the curriculum is presented as one more technique for making it available to those children who need it. If no perceptual training program is available, then use of the modified curriculum may make this training accessible to some children who otherwise would be denied it. If some ongoing program of perceptual training is available, it may be enriched and supplemented by perceptual training through these suggested curriculum modifications.

At present, the regular classroom is the place where perceptual training is needed most urgently. The vast majority of children with learning disorders are in regular classrooms. If they get help they will get it there. Most of these children do not have problems which are so severe that they should be placed in special classrooms even under ideal conditions, and present conditions are far from ideal. Not enough special classes exist to meet even the needs of children with severe problems, and this situation is likely to prevail for years to come. No one knows how many children in regular classrooms need some form of perceptual training, but no doubt these children are in our classrooms and they are there in large numbers; estimates range from one-tenth to one-third of the school population. If the regular classroom does not provide help, most of these children will go without it.

The use of certain modified curriculum activities for perceptual training should be helpful also to special-education teachers, for these teachers face the same problem as the regular teacher where perceptual training is concerned: The academic training and perceptual training tend to compete for time. Two of the four sample curriculum units in the book, therefore, have been designed primarily for a special-education classroom setting; both of the other units, with only slight modifications, would be suitable for special-education classes. Conversely, the special-education material illustrates techniques which could be adapted to regular classes.

The latter part of Chapter 1 consists of a statement of a theory of perceptual development and a discussion of principles for modifying curriculum activities to promote perceptual training. The four chapters which follow are presented as applications of the theory and principles. Each contains a unit of study which is designed to convey academic subject matter along with related perceptual training activities. These units are for illustrative purposes only. Each unit is for a different grade level and academic area as follows:

Chapter 2: 5th Grade, *Social Studies* (This chapter contains a special social-studies project; it is not properly a unit of study.)
Chapter 3: 1st Grade, *Language Arts*
Chapter 4: Intermediate Elementary Educable Mentally Retarded, *Science*
Chapter 5: Secondary Educable Mentally Retarded, *Vocational Training*.

The unit activities are concrete examples of modifying the presentation of typical curriculum material to provide the student with academic learning experiences and remedial activities simultaneously. Explanations of how a given activity leads to remediation accompany the description of that activity, except where repetitions would be merely tiresome.

That the teacher view the four curriculum units as examples of applications of theory and principles is extremely important. You, the teacher, should make your own curriculum modifications out of your own insights into children's needs and from your own knowledge of just what remediation a given activity may contribute to those needs. A teacher should not attempt perceptual training on a "cookbook" basis; rather, he should know what a given activity is expected to accomplish and how it accomplishes it. The four units are aids to demonstrate how theory and principles may be applied. The units will have served their purpose for you, the teacher, whenever they illustrate principles which you will come to use when you yourself plan or modify other units.

The approach presented in this book is offered only as a beginning step toward combining perceptual training with curriculum activities. The intention is to suggest how such a combination can be brought about, rather than to prescribe specific programs. Hopefully, the ultimate goal of extracting perceptual training from the curriculum will be realized as creative teachers set their imaginations to the task. The purpose of this book will have been achieved if it stimulates those teachers to attempt the task, and if it offers a few guidelines along the way.

A THEORY OF PERCEPTUAL DEVELOPMENT

For a comprehensive theoretical basis of the approach to perceptual training used in this book, the reader is referred to *The Slow*

The Problem and an Approach

Learner in the Classroom (Kephart, 1960) and "Motor Generalizations in Space and Time" (Dunsing and Kephart, 1965). Only a broad outline of theory is attempted in this chapter. Emphasis is placed upon those aspects which seem especially important to classroom teachers.

THE STRUCTURED SELF AND THE STRUCTURED WORLD

If a child is to receive and organize information from the world about him, he himself must be organized or structured internally. A child who is disorganized internally cannot be expected to organize information which comes from some source outside himself. If, for example, he has not developed an inner awareness of "left" and "right," he will have trouble distinguishing the letter "b" from the letter "d," because the only difference between these two letters is a difference in direction. If he has a poor internal awareness of "up" as different from "down," he may be unable to tell the letter "p" from the letter "d" or to distinguish "b" from "q." Without inner organization, the child's world will be confused, and the information he receives from that world will not be dependable or meaningful. For this reason, it is often said of children with perceptual problems, "They do not see what we see, hear what we hear, or experience the world as we experience it." Perceptual difficulties arise when the child's internal structure is missing, incomplete, or distorted. He must develop an internally structured self in order to function in a structured world.

Structure, in general, denotes an orderly arrangement of interrelated parts to make up a whole. In any structure, each part must perform its function in relation to all other parts and their functions. An automobile, for example, is a highly structured piece of equipment. It is made up of many parts which must function together if the whole car is to do its work of transporting you along the road. It has a frame and four wheels which roll. An engine produces the power for movement, and a power train (transmission, drive shaft, differential, axles) connects the power to the wheels. An accelerator varies the speed, and a brake stops the movement. A steering system controls direction. All these elements have particular functions to perform if the car is to operate properly, and each part must perform its function in relation to the others: The engine must be started before the wheels turn; the car must be in motion before the steering system can control direction; the brake is not applied when the accelerator is increasing speed, and so on.

The driver controls the automobile; he makes it do his bidding. Drivers are made, not born. As a driver must learn to drive, as he must learn to monitor and control the complex automobile with all its dynamic and flexible potentialities, so must the child learn to monitor and control the far more complex equipment of his body. The development of the structured self may be compared to the training of a driver: When the structured self has developed, the child is "in the driver's seat" with respect to his body. The structured self is that internal awareness whereby the child knows his body and its potentials and limitations, and controls that body so that it functions to serve him.

The automobile is a structured piece of equipment because it is put together on the assembly line in such a way that all the parts function together. In a similar manner, the child must structure himself into a functional whole. He begins with the parts; his task is to put the parts together into his own unique but structured self. The child structures himself by interacting with the orderly world in which he lives. From this interaction he receives information about the world and about himself in relation to the world. He uses this information to develop an inner awareness of his own body in relation to space and time. This inner awareness lets him know where and what his body parts are, how they work together, and what they can or cannot do. His structured self becomes the reference point, the starting point, the "zero-point," from which he relates and orders the elements of the space-time world.

When this inner structure or organization is well developed and functioning, the child is in charge of a magnificent instrument — his own body. He can cause his hand to perform highly skilled tasks without concentrating on the movements; he can keep his attention on the task itself. He can vary the tasks over an astounding range, because he can bring to bear literally an infinite number of specific manipulations out of a vast storehouse of flexible movement patterns. He can look at an object some distance away and know in which direction his eyes are pointing, and also how far the object is from him. In a split second he can comprehend its shape, color, and texture, and he has some idea about how heavy it is and what kind of sound it would make if he struck it with his hand. He can move from place to place with smooth and rhythmic motions without thinking about or planning each motion, because these actions, too, come out of his storehouse of flexible patterns. He can listen, and in the process gain information from the sounds which come from a friend's mouth. He can bring into a harmonious whole the air in his lungs and the muscles in his vocal cords, tongue, lips, jaws, cheeks, with a precision of timing that staggers the imagination; and he can use the end product to tell you of the things he sees, knows, loves, and fears. He can do these things and a million more because he is a structured self in a structured world.

The child who is this well structured internally is able to take part in the perceptual process. He can receive information through his various sense avenues, and he can interpret it, because his own internal structure gives him a basis for organizing the information.

As a simple example of how internal organization is used to organize incoming information, consider a child as he looks at a tree some 50 or so feet from himself. He knows the direction to the tree only because he knows the direction in which his own head and eyes are pointing. He knows the direction of his head and eyes only from his internal structure. His neck muscles produce information about the location of his head; the muscles which control eye movements produce information about the location of his eyes with respect to his head. Since he is organized internally, this information from these particular muscles tells him the direction of his gaze. Without this internal organization he will not know with accuracy where his eyes are pointing, and so will lack essential information for learning relationships among objects in space.

His internal structure tells him more about the tree than its direction. From this same internal structure, he can make fairly accurate estimates of the distance to the tree and the time needed for him to walk that distance. His previous interactions with the world have helped him develop internalized information about relative distances and times. Visual information from the tree can thus be measured against his internal scale of distance and time.

From the educator's point of view, the development of internal structure is a matter of the highest importance. In reading, a child must receive and organize complex visual information from printed symbols on a page. Successful performance of this task demands a highly developed internal structure. Similarly, arithmetic involves the vicarious manipulation of relationships among objects in space. Listening to a story being read requires receiving auditory stimulation and translating that stimulation into meaningful patterns. Drawing a simple form requires the ability to organize the form internally and to translate this internal organization into a series of movements which take place in both time and space. Writing demands a similar but more complex ability. In all these and countless other school tasks, successful achievement depends directly upon the child's internal structure.

This all-important internal structure does not occur automatically; it develops in an orderly way as the child interacts with his environment, and as he receives and processes information from his interactions. The development begins at birth and is generally fairly complete at around 8 years of age. If the development is hampered in any way, the internal structure is likely to show some deficits, and perception may be impaired. For example, an understaffed children's institution may result in lack of opportunity to interact with the environment, and development may suffer. Or the environment itself may be so impoverished that it offers restricted opportunities for meaningful interactions, as is often the case in culturally deprived areas. On the other end of the socio-economic scale, a toddler may be forced to restrict his explorations of his environment because he is a lively threat to prized or fragile ornaments or household furnishings. Anything which interrupts or interferes with a child's explorations and interactions can affect adversely the development of the structured self. An extended hospital confinement, a slight injury to the central nervous system, too much confinement to the playpen, or any other restrictions upon free movement and spontaneous exploration may impede the development of internal structure.

THE MOTOR BASIS OF INTERNAL STRUCTURE

The infant's interactions with his environment produce information about that environment and about the infant himself. This information which comes from his explorations and interactions must be processed in some fashion. Without processing, it is nothing more than a mass of raw sensory stimuli. The interactions produce both internal information about what is happening to the infant and external information about what is going on outside of him. In interacting with the world, therefore, the infant is alternately and progressively learning about his own body and the world in which his body is functioning. Initially, he is thought to learn something of his body; this initial body knowledge gives him a basis for learning something from the world at large.

The infant's earliest learnings are motor learnings. The first information he learns to process is motor information; that is, the internal information which is produced by his own movements. Motor information comes from the vestibular sense (equilibrium) and kinesthetic receptors inside the body. These kinesthetic receptors are in the muscles, tendons, and joints. They provide a continuous feedback to the central nervous system about movement and position of the body parts.

The Problem and an Approach

Motor information is also the first information which is organized as part of the internal structure. Furthermore, as motor information becomes structured it provides a basis, or frame of reference, for organizing information from the senses. Visual information and auditory information are organized and structured as they are matched to previously organized motor information.

This internal organization of motor information will be called the *motor base*. Motor base refers to an internal and organized awareness of the body which develops from processing motor information; the parts of the body, their relative location and interrelatedness, and their movements and possibilities for movements. The motor base is the primary internal structure to which other sensory information is subsequently matched and structured. This matching of other sensory information to the motor base is discussed more fully later.

The motor base does not become fully developed before it is used to organize visual and auditory information. It develops in stages. Vision, for example, may be organized by matching visual information repeatedly to the motor base at progressive stages; however, a partially organized motor base will result in a similar partial organization of vision. Both motor base and vision will develop together in progressive stages, but at each stage the organization of the motor base normally precedes visual organization. The important point is that the motor base is the foundation structure upon which all other perceptual information is in turn structured. For this reason, certain motor activities often play an important role in remediation of perceptual problems.

DEVELOPING THE MOTOR BASE

The infant's beginning movements are total movements, usually involving the whole body. Typically, a sweep of movement from head to foot occurs. Such total movement is called undifferentiated movement; no one part makes distinctive and purposeful movements. The movement of an arm, for example, is not distinguished as separate and distinct from the total movement of the body as a whole. The general effect is a mass of unorganized movement where everything seems to "go off at once." Obviously, this mass of undifferentiated movement is of little value for exploring the world and obtaining information.

The first step is to differentiate, distinguish, or separate out the individual body parts and their movements from the total or undifferentiated mass of movement. Coghill (1929) has shown that the differentiation of body parts proceeds in sequence and in two directions: (1) the proximo-distal direction (from the center of the body outward), and (2) the cephalo-caudal direction (from head to toe). In the proximo-distal sequence, the infant first distinguishes those parts which are closest to the vertical midline of his body; then he differentiates in order the other parts lying progressively farther from his center. Thus, he first differentiates his trunk, next his shoulders, then his upper arms, elbows, forearms, wrists, hands, and finally his fingers — all in sequence and in a direction from the midline outward. In the cephalo-caudal sequence, he first differentiates his head and neck, next his shoulders and trunk, then his knees, legs, ankles, feet and toes — again, all in sequence and in a head-to-foot direction.

Kephart (1960), drawing upon Coghill's work, has emphasized the importance for the educator of this sequential development. In many children with learning disorders, the development has either not been completed, or some parts have not been differentiated in the proper sequence. Without realizing it, a teacher may even complicate and increase the problem. In kindergarten or first grade, a child may be required to use his fingers in complex manipulation of crayons or pencils before he has differentiated his hand, wrist, elbow, or even his whole arm. Under these conditions, what skill he manages to force upon his fingers develops as an isolated or "splinter" skill. Such isolated skills are termed "splinter" skills because they are not part of a flexible pattern of movement; they are said to be "splintered off" from the motor base, and they tend to be highly restricted movements which are capable only of specific and rigid operations.

The problem of splintering is intensified when the fingers are forced into action before the preceding parts are differentiated and organized into flexible movement patterns. Motor problems may persist beyond the early grades because the splintering may prevent completion of the sequential differentiation. The writer has a vivid recollection of a 9-year-old boy with learning disorders who, in writing at the chalkboard, kept his entire arm rigid while making all movements for writing from the shoulder only. His arm, elbow, wrist, and hand all moved as one stiff unit. This boy had scarcely differentiated any parts of his arm beyond his shoulder. Incomplete or improperly sequenced differentiation of body

The Problem and an Approach

parts can result not only in such specific school problems as the foregoing, but can also interfere with the development of the motor base itself.

As the child differentiates his body parts and their movements, as he becomes better acquainted with his body and how the parts move, he must next recombine, or integrate, the parts into flexible, purposeful, and generalized movement patterns. In integrating the separate movements, he must also deal with the reflexes, combining them into the flexible patterns. Reflex movements are specific movements caused by specific stimuli; they are therefore restricted and rigid in their patterns. To be useful, they must be broadened and incorporated into functional patterns. Starting with a mass of unorganized movement, the child first separates movements from each other; he then combines these movements with the reflexes, and puts them back together as organized patterns. Most important, the new patterns must be *generalized movement patterns* rather than specific, narrow and rigid skills.

A generalized movement pattern is highly flexible. It may make use of an unlimited variety of muscular movements. In the simple act of reaching for an object, one may begin reaching no matter what the starting position of the hand. If the hand is at the side, reaching forward from that position will require the activation of certain specific muscles; if the hand happens to be elevated, an entirely different set of muscles will be brought into play. If a child has developed generalized movement patterns, he has an inner awareness of all the possibilities for movement at any given moment. Generalized movement patterns enable him to draw upon this inner awareness and to bring into action whatever specific muscles are needed for a given task. He does not need to rely only upon one set of muscles for a particular task; he can set the generalized pattern in motion, and the specific muscles are activated as elements of the pattern. For a given movement, then, the well-developed child does not have to make a detailed analysis of which muscles need activating; instead, he brings the pattern into play, and the muscular activity follows naturally and smoothly.

Generalized movement patterns let a child focus his attention upon the goal of his movements; he is not distracted by the necessity of attending to the production of each specific movement. A well-organized child can walk without attending to moving first one foot and then the other. He can keep his attention on where he is going instead of on the movements he must make to get there. Furthermore, he can vary the manner of locomotion as he wishes or as the situation demands: He can walk, run, hop, skip, or lope, and he can detour obstacles in his path without having to reorganize his movements with each break in the pattern.

The difference between generalized movement patterns and splinter skills may be illustrated by examining the manner in which children write. Some children seem to learn writing as a collection of detailed and highly specific splinter skills. Each element of each letter is made as if the specific movement to make that element were memorized. At the chalkboard, the wrist is rested on the board, duplicating as nearly as possible the position of the hand when the child was seated at a desk or table. Writing movements typically are slow and jerky, each movement requiring recall and planning before it is executed. With so much attention demanded by the movements for writing, one can easily see that the child can give little attention to what is being written.

The child with a well-developed motor base, on the other hand, can employ generalized movement patterns in writing, and can keep his attention on what he is writing rather than on how he makes the movements for writing. For the task of writing, he has available a generalized pattern of movements from which he can draw an unlimited number of specific movements as needed. This child can write at the chalkboard with a radically different set of muscles and movements from those he uses at his desk. The movements will flow smoothly because each movement is part of an organized pattern of movement; any individual movement does not have to be planned and executed separately. The development of generalized movement patterns is so important for learning that it can hardly be overemphasized.

Development of generalized movement patterns arises directly out of the following conditions:

1. Greatly varied interactions with a rich and varied environment.
2. Differentiation of body parts in the proper sequence (proximo-distal and cephalo-caudal).
3. Integration of the separate parts and their movements into generalized movement patterns.

In interacting with his environment, the child is, in effect, conducting countless experiments which help him learn what his body can do. A variety of experiments in a rich environment reveals to him the enormous range of movements which is possible with his body parts, either as individual parts or in combination. From this

The Problem and an Approach

experimentation comes differentiation and integration of parts as the child discovers the parts and experiments with the wide range of movements they make.

In summary, developing the motor base means developing an inner awareness of all the possibilities for movements that are available for each body part and for all possible combinations of parts. The motor base develops as the child makes a wide range of experiments with a rich and diverse environment. From these experiments, the child differentiates his body parts in proper sequence and then integrates the parts into generalized movement patterns. From this differentiation and integration comes an inner awareness of the body and all its potential for movement. The organized inner awareness is termed a motor base because it is the base upon which subsequent organization is built. To the extent that the motor base is truly an inner awareness, to the extent that it is "wired in" so to speak, further movements and explorations can be made without requiring the child to focus his attention on the movements themselves. He is free to attend to the goals of movement and exploration, and thus is better able to receive and process information.

STRUCTURING SPACE

In the entire universe, no object is right or left, up or down, before or after, *in and of itself*. These terms denote relationships, and relationships require a point of reference in order to have meaning. If two people face each other, what is "right" for one is "left" for the other. For these directional terms to have meaning, they must be referred to an observer who becomes the reference point. The child structures the universe initially by referring objects to his own body. By using his body as a reference point, he is able to impose his internal structure upon the external world and thus to determine relationships among the objects and events in that world.

The child develops an internal awareness of left and right from his internal awareness that his body has two sides. The inner awareness is called *laterality*, and laterality is part of the motor base. It should be emphasized strongly that laterality is an inner awareness of left as different from right. It is therefore something more than just knowing the names of the two sides. A child may be able to name the sides accurately and still not possess laterality.

Laterality develops as the infant solves the fundamental problems associated with maintaining the posture and balance of his body. In shifting his body to assume various postures and in maintaining his balance, he comes to grips with the one constant in his world: the force of gravity. This force is always in the same direction ("down"), and this constant direction serves as a dependable reference for sorting out the various parts of the body. In fighting with gravity to maintain balance and posture, the child must continuously activate sets of opposing muscles. If he sways to the left, he tenses muscles on the right side of his body to prevent a fall. From many similar experiences he becomes aware that his body has two separate sides, and that the two sides work together.

In similar fashion, the relative location of body parts along a vertical line promotes an inner awareness of "up" as contrasted to "down." The feet become associated with "down," and parts closer to the head are associated with "up." This inner awareness of up and down is termed *verticality*. In like manner, parts in front of the body are distinguished from parts behind. The net effect is as if the body were bisected by three planes as follows:

1. One vertical plane dividing the body into two lateral halves: left and right.
2. One horizontal plane dividing the body into two parts: upper and lower.
3. One vertical plane dividing the body into two parts: front and rear.

The internal awareness of left as different from right, up as different from down, and front as different from rear has the effect of giving the child his own personal set of three-dimensional space coordinates. Information coming from the world can be located in terms of the child's three-dimensional awareness of his own body. The child first learns to organize that part of the world which is within arm's reach. An object is touched, and from the internal organization it is determined that the object is, for example, on the child's right front and that it is about chest-high. Touching an object will give information about where that object is located only if the child knows where his hand was when the object was touched. His internal organization lets him know where his hand is, and from this knowledge he knows the relative position of the object he touched. In this experience of locating by touch, the child is locating objects outside himself by projecting his own internal organization outward upon objects in space. Through such pro-

The Problem and an Approach

jections, the near space within arm's reach becomes structured. As he learns to match the visual information from looking at an object to the tactual experience of touching the object, he comes to locate objects at near point from visual information alone. When this development has taken place, he then can expand his near-point organization, and can locate objects beyond arm's reach. In this way, he begins to structure space by structuring the objects that fill space. The child's structuring of space, then, depends upon his development of his own internal structure and the projection of that structure outward upon the world around him.

Space is organized as the child receives information from the world and matches that information to his internally organized motor base. This matching of information is known as the *perceptual-motor match*. According to the theory presented here, the incoming information for perception is matched to the motor base; as incoming information is matched to a structured motor base, the incoming information itself becomes structured. The information comes in a variety of forms through the various sense avenues. Through the perceptual-motor match, all this information becomes structured into meaningful wholes. Without structure, the information is little more than a jumble of sensory stimulation.

Visual information, auditory information, and tactual-kinesthetic information are the major types of incoming information with which the perceptual-motor match is concerned. Exploring just one object may produce information simultaneously from eyes, ears, and muscles. The information from each of these three sources is different information, because sight is different from sound, and muscles are different from both. However, each source gives its different information about the same object. A child may *see* the corners, surfaces, and edges of a block, and he may *feel* the corners, surfaces, and edges at the same time. His hands and eyes give him distinctly different information, but a connection exists between the two: The information comes from the same source. An edge "looks sharp" because it "feels sharp," and the child has learned that certain aspects of "feeling" give a corresponding aspect of "looking." Similar obvious comparisons may be made with respect to how objects "sound."

Through countless experiments, a child learns to organize incoming information from the three major sources by relating this information to his motor base. From his motor base he knows where his hand is located at a given moment. If his hand touches an object and explores the object, he knows where the object is located because the tactual-kinesthetic information is referred to the motor base. From these explorations he determines both the location of the object in space and also the internal relationships of the elements which make up the object. If the child explores the object visually at the same time, the movements of his eyes come in time to correspond to hand and finger movements; in this fashion eye movements and hand movements become coordinated. The visual impression of the object becomes organized as the visual information is matched to the information simultaneously referred to the motor base through the hand and fingers. If, in exploring the object, the child bangs it on the floor and makes a sound, auditory information is produced. As sound becomes related to visual and tactual-kinesthetic impressions, more information about the object is matched to the motor base. The location of the object becomes determined from auditory clues as well as tactual-kinesthetic and visual clues, and tactual and visual impressions of relative "hardness" become associated with the sound the object makes. Visual, auditory, and tactual-kinesthetic impressions thus become organized by being matched to a previously organized motor base; in the process, the sensory avenues become coordinated and interrelated.

If perception is understood as organizing or structuring incoming information into meaningful patterns, then the role of the motor base in the perceptual process becomes of fundamental importance. The motor base provides the initial structure. Incoming sensory information is structured as it is matched to the structured motor base. A child's structured motor base provides him with an accurate knowledge of what is happening to his body, the parts of his body, and the movements the parts make. The movements he makes in exploring his world are now organized movements. Visual information and auditory information become organized by matching to organized movements; the organized movements provide a means of linking visual and auditory information to the motor base. Through countless repetitions of the perceptual-motor match, the visual and auditory sense avenues themselves become structured; at this point, the motor base need no longer be involved directly in each and every act of seeing and hearing. The motor base is used to structure vision and hearing; once this has been done, the eyes and ears are able to receive and organize information directly.

If the sense avenues are not structured, they do not give the child consistent, dependable, or veridical information about the world. If a child is to function in school, he must be able to per-

The Problem and an Approach

ceive form. Words are composed of letters, and each letter is a visual symbol. To recognize the symbols, the child must be able to receive organized information through his eyes. If his vision is not organized, he will not be able to organize the visual information which the symbols are supposed to convey to him. Arithmetic demands that he be able to perceive relationships among objects in space, but if his vision lacks structure, he will be unable to perceive the basic relationships among objects which are right in front of his eyes, to say nothing of the more abstract perception of relationships when concrete objects are removed.

The coordination of eye and hand is of such importance to educators that special note of this aspect of the perceptual-motor match will be made here. This development is in two stages: The hand-eye stage develops first and the eye-hand stage follows later. In the hand-eye stage, the movements of the hand tend to attract the attention of the eyes. The hand will be moving, and the eyes, almost by accident, will be attracted by and begin to follow this movement. In time, the child realizes that the motor information from hand movements and the visual information from his eyes as they follow those movements are actually two sources of information about the same event: the movement of the hand. The information from the eyes is matched to the information from the movements of the hand. In this hand-eye stage the hand leads the eye; that is, the eye merely follows hand movements. Eye-hand coordination develops after hand-eye coordination. In this latter stage, the eye can now fix upon a certain object, and the hand can be brought to the object.

From the foregoing it can be seen that the motor base serves as a vehicle for organizing the information for perception during the time when perception is developing. Once perception has developed, the motor aspect can drop out, and information can be organized more directly. As you read these printed words, you are receiving visual information which you readily combine into meaningful information. You are organizing visual symbols into forms and patterns which give you information about concepts which the writer is trying to convey. As you read these lines, you no longer need be aware that they read from left to right. These words consist of lines in space, and you readily organize the lines which make up each letter. You do this without going through the laborious process of comparing each bit of visual information to your internally organized motor base. You do not, for example, need to refer each letter of each word to your motor base to determine whether it is rightside up or upside down. You are able to do all this, however, because you did develop a stable motor base, and you did learn to use that motor base to organize the information you received through your various sense avenues.

Because your sense avenues are organized or structured, you are able to organize your surroundings readily and with astonishing efficiency. You can take a quick glance around you, and everything fits together. You can lift your eyes from this book and look at the table or desk at which you are sitting. You perceive it as a table or desk. You know how the surface will feel without touching it. You know that the corners are sharp or round simply by looking; you need not touch them to know this. You know by looking that the material in the desk or table is solid and will not sag if you press your hand down on it; you need no longer experiment to discover it. You know that if you drop this book on your desk a certain sound will occur, and that if you set a coffee cup on it a different sound will be forthcoming. Merely by looking, you can know all this and much more about what is before you at this moment. You can shut your eyes and retain a good mental picture of the location of most of the objects in the room. You can organize your surroundings this efficiently because when you were a child you performed a thousand experiments where you matched incoming information to your motor base. The child who has not succeeded in structuring his sense avenues has trouble organizing his surroundings. Space, for him, does not hold together consistently as it does for you.

STRUCTURING TIME

Space and time are related. As a child must learn to structure space, so must he learn to structure time. The relationship between space and time is such that the child must learn to move readily from one to the other and to interchange one for the other. A simple example may point up the relationship between space and time, the need to structure both of these worlds, and the necessity for moving back and forth from one to the other.

A child who has developed a structured space world and a structured time world can, among other things, perceive and draw a square. A square consists of four equal lines in specific relationship. Perceiving the form called "square" requires the ability to deal with lines and relationships as they exist in *space*. On the other hand, if the child draws a square, he cannot draw all four

The Problem and an Approach

lines in the same instant; *he must, therefore, transfer the form in space into the world of time* if he is to draw it. He draws the first line, then the second, third, and fourth lines; each line is produced at a time which is different from the time in which any other line is produced. As he draws any one line he must hold onto the form as it exists in space. He must function in the time world while holding onto a form which he perceives in the space world. To accomplish even this simple task, a child must have both a structured space world and a structured time world, and he must be able to move freely from one world to the other.

The behavior of many children suggests strongly that their time world lacks structure. A child may attempt copying tasks at great speed as if he is trying to do the task in "zero time," and in this way avoid the necessity of functioning in the time world. Seemingly, he can deal with only one element of the task at a time; in dealing with this one element he "loses" the other elements. In drawing a square, he may produce one line, but lose the other three as he deals with the one. He tries to solve the time problem by making extremely rapid movements, as if by moving rapidly he can finish the task before the elements elude him.

The same lack of temporal structure is seen in a child who cannot perform a sequence of activities. Johnny may be told to do three things: erase the board, empty the wastebasket, and take a note to the principal. If all these instructions are given to him before he starts any one task, he may do the first (or the last), and then be at a loss as to what comes next. Events take place in time; time must be structured if those events are to hold together or have dependable relationships.

Dunsing and Kephart (1965) point out three aspects of time, and compare each aspect to a corresponding aspect of space. The three aspects of time are synchrony, rhythm, and sequence. These terms are defined as follows:

1. *Synchrony* is "controlled simultaneity of movement designed for a purpose."
2. *Rhythm* is "a regular succession of repeated synchronous acts designed for a purpose."
3. *Sequence* is "an ordering in time of dissimilar objects or events."[1]

---

[1]Permission granted by Special Child Publications, Inc., 4535 Union Bay Place N.E., Seattle, Washington 98105, for the use of quotations from Jack D. Dunsing's and Newell C. Kephart's chapter, "Motor Generalizations in Space and Time" printed in Vol. 1 of the annual series *Learning Disorders*, edited by Jerome Hellmuth.

These three "dimensions" of time are developed and structured in much the same way that space is developed and structured: Both time and space structures grow out of the developing motor base.

Synchrony is related to "nowness"; that is, if the terms "before" and "after" have meaning, that meaning can only be in relation to a point in time we call "now." Synchrony provides such a point in time ("now") to which other events may be related. This awareness that a "now" exists in time develops initially from synchronous body movements. The earliest awareness of "now" arises from the child's efforts to balance himself as he assumes various postures. If, in attempting any given posture, his body tends to become unbalanced, he can maintain balance by making corrective movements. Such corrective movements to maintain balance must be made at the precise moment when balance is threatened; they must be made "now" and not "later." In this way, a starting point on the child's time scale develops from his body movements. *Just as his body becomes the starting point for ordering objects in space, so his body becomes the same kind of starting point for ordering events in time.*

If synchrony provides a starting point or "zero point" on the time scale, rhythm may be said to furnish the scale itself. From rhythmic movements the child develops an awareness of time divided into units which correspond to the inches on a yardstick. In creeping on hands and knees, for example, the infant is moving from one point to another in space. His movements typically are rhythmical, smooth, and beautifully coordinated. As he negotiates a given amount of space he also negotiates a given and corresponding amount of time. Both space and time are measured in terms of the movements he makes to cover that much space and that much time. Perhaps no example is clearer than this to point up the close connection between space, time, and body movements.

As synchrony has been presented as the starting point on the time scale, and rhythm has been compared with the scale itself, so sequence may be described as the form, or pattern, of time which corresponds to form perception of objects in space. Objects exist in space, and their relationships to one another form patterns. Events exist in time, and, in a somewhat similar fashion, their relationships in time form patterns. It has been shown that the child's initial location of objects in space is made possible by his own internal body structure. A similar point can be made with respect to his locating and structuring events in time. As objects

The Problem and an Approach 23

are first located in space by movements from one object to another, so events are located and organized in time in terms of the body movements which intervene between one event and another.

FROM THEORY TO REMEDIATION

As an infant, the child began functioning at the first, or *motor level*, where his main source of information about the world was from his motor interactions. He then began to develop a motor base, and to move to the second, or *motor-perceptual level* where incoming data for perception were matched to the motor base. At this second level, for example, the hand leads the eye. Next, he advances to the third level, where incoming perceptual data can lead motor activities; in one instance, the eye now leads and guides the hand. The third level is known as the *perceptual-motor level*. The fourth level is the *perceptual level*, where incoming sensory data are organized into meaningful patterns without overt reference to the motor base.

Once a child is functioning adequately at the perceptual level, he is ready to proceed to the development of *concepts*. He begins building concepts from a number of percepts; in this fifth or *perceptual-conceptual level*, concepts depend upon percepts. The sixth level is the purely *conceptual level*, where conceptualizing may take place independently of any overt perceptual activity. The seventh, and final, level is the *conceptual-perceptual level*, where perception is conditioned by previously developed concepts.

Children with learning disorders often demonstrate, upon careful diagnosis, certain behaviors which clearly indicate that they have not developed a solid internal structure, and that this lack of structure adversely affects their ability to organize their world and the information which comes from that world. Failure to achieve adequate structure may occur at any level of development. At the lowest level, the motor development may be inadequate, thus affecting the structure of higher levels. The perceptual-motor match may be faulty, resulting in inadequate structuring of one or more of the sensory avenues: visual, auditory, tactual-kinesthetic. Development of structure also may be adequate up to a point, and fail to take place beyond that point. Wherever the development of the internal structure breaks down, a corresponding inability to organize the external world may be expected. Children who fail to develop a functioning inner structure and project that structure outward upon their environment are truly "perceptually handicapped." To the extent that they can be helped to develop an internal structure, they may be released from their handicap, and be made more susceptible to the typical academic demands placed upon them.

Stated in its baldest form, the theory outlined would hold that the fundamental problem in many children with learning disorders is a lack of inner structure, and that this lack of structure prevents a child from receiving and/or processing information in a dependable way. Inadequate structure shows up in a variety of ways in the classroom. Copying from the chalkboard is extremely difficult for many children with poor visual-motor structure. Shifting the eyes from chalkboard to desk involves rapid movement of eyes and prompt refocusing. In attempting this quite basic task, a child may search for the place on his paper, and, in the act of searching, forget what he saw on the board. He shifts back to the board, finds again what he just lost, shifts again to his paper, begins a new search for the proper place, and possibly loses the copy again. Such a child may have visual acuity of 20/20 and still lack an adequately structured and functional vision.

Other children are in trouble whenever they must add motor activity to any task. Writing requires of these children an excessive effort and concentration merely to produce the characters. With so much attention upon the production of the writing movements, little is left to concentrate upon what is being written. For others the reverse is true; they must still add the motor to guide the visual. These children may need a hand or finger to guide their eyes while reading; without this crutch their eyes cannot sweep smoothly over the page.

The problems associated with inadequate structure are complex and endlessly varied. The examples given suggest only a few of the difficulties. By careful observation of a child's behavior, a teacher may, however, make some dependable judgments regarding just where structure seems inadequate, and what remediation is in order. The school psychologist may have information which would help locate areas of functioning which need attention. Various standardized test instruments often yield information which will suggest specific deficits of structure. The following tests are especially helpful, and may be administered by teachers:

The Purdue Perceptual-Motor Survey (Roach and Kephart, 1966)
The Marianne Frostig Developmental Test of Visual Perception (Frostig, 1963)

The Problem and an Approach

Screening Tests for Identifying Children with Specific Language Disability (Slingerland, 1964)
Durrell Analysis of Reading Difficulty (Durrell, 1955).

In using these tests to assess areas of structural difficulty, the teacher should analyze the subtest scores and the child's pattern of performance on each subtest. Total scores on any one test will not be too helpful in the type of analysis suggested here. Rather, a comparison of performances on several subtests often will point to specific areas where structural deficits are causing trouble. For example, one Frostig subtest is named "Spatial Relations." The test items require the child to reproduce configurations of increasing complexity; the configurations consist of short connected lines with abrupt changes in direction. If a child scores low on this test, his problem could be a lack of directionality (caused by poor laterality), inadequate visual structure, inadequate motor coordination (which interferes with his ability to reproduce the figures), poor visual-motor coordination, difficulty with form perception, or a combination of these. By comparing performance on this subtest with that on other subtests, certain items will come to the fore as indicators of the basic structural problem. If the Frostig "Figure-Ground" test is passed, one may eliminate tentatively the possibility that form perception is the main problem. If laterality items on the Purdue Perceptual-Motor Survey are scored low, then further checking on directionality is indicated. If "Eye-Motor Coordination" (Frostig) and "Perceptual-Motor Match" (Purdue) are low, then a lack of visual-motor structure is suggested. By checking clues from one subtest against clues from other subtests, a pattern begins to emerge.

The Durrell and Slingerland tests have many helpful subtests. The Durrell gives grade norms for comprehension on oral and silent reading as well as listening. If a child is much higher on listening comprehension (where vision is eliminated from the task) than on reading (where vision is basic to the task), a further check on vision obviously is indicated. The "Ocular Control" items on the Purdue Survey may give some decisive information in this case. The Slingerland test includes reading at both far-point and near-point, and it also has some extremely helpful items where reading and writing are deliberately interrupted by gross motor activities.

The various subtests contain a variety of items where tasks are designed to involve different sensory and motor activities. Following the clues from these test items will help the teacher locate the areas where structure has broken down and is causing learning problems. Teacher observations of behavior patterns are essential to analysis. The tests discussed above are suggested as aids to systematic observation, but not as a substitute. The teacher may prefer other test instruments than these listed; many tests will yield much the same information. Regardless of the method of assessment, the key suggestion is that the child's pattern of performance be studied in an effort to discover the basic problems in his structure of himself, his structure of his environment, and his structure of the avenues through which his environment is perceived.

In those cases where lack of structure is interfering with learning, the remediation logically should focus upon the fundamental problem: the lack of structure. If the teacher takes this assertion seriously, then the remediation of some academic problems will involve activities which are bound to seem strange or even out of place in the classroom. An almost unspoken assumption is that the business of education is conducted only through books, words, paper, pencils, chalk, audio-visuals, field trips, and the like. The suggestion to employ activities to promote balance, posture, laterality, body image, eye-hand coordination, and similar perceptual training carries with it the faint suspicion that one is proposing something that is not quite academic. Nevertheless, the assertion still is made: If lack of structure is causing learning problems, the obvious remedy is to introduce activities which will promote structure.

All that has been presented so far has been described as theory, but this theory is buttressed by a wealth of clinical experience and solid research. From the considerable literature on the subject, the study of Hagin, Silver, and Hersh (1965) will be summarized as a fairly typical and rather dramatic example of the results of perceptual training.

Hagin, Silver, and Hersh conducted an experiment with forty boys (ages 8-11 years), all of whom were referred to the Bellevue Mental Hygiene Clinic because of behavior and school learning problems. The boys were divided into two groups, and each child was paired with a corresponding child in the other group in terms of age, IQ, psychiatric diagnosis, and neurological status. The experimental group received 6 months of training in "perceptual stimulation"; the control group received individual sessions of conventional teaching from a basal reading series. Each child in each group received training or teaching for two 45-minute periods each week during the 6-month period. Test-retest measures

The Problem and an Approach 27

revealed that the experimental group (which received perceptual training) made significant gains on the Jastak Wide Range Achievement Test and on the Reading Section of the appropriate levels of the Metropolitan Achievement Tests. The control group (which received individual conventional teaching) did not make significant improvement on either of these measures. In addition, the experimental group made significant improvement on the Bender-Gestalt Test and the Right-Left Discrimination Test; however, no significant improvement was made on Wepman's Test of Auditory Discrimination, Goodenough Drawing, or the Finger Schema Test. The control group did not make significant improvement on any of the psychological measures. In discussing their experiment, these authorities offer the following significant comment: "It is suggested that perceptual training stimulates neurological maturation to a level appropriate for reading. This implies a relationship between perception and language abilities. If we look for a common denominator in our methods of perceptual stimulation, *we are impressed that problems in spatial and temporal orientation underlie them all,* be they visual, auditory, tactual, or kinesthetic." (Italics mine)[2]

From this study, the point which should be underscored is this: Perceptual training, a "nonacademic" set of activities, resulted in statistically significant academic gains. Equally important, perceptual training resulted in significant gains on various psychological tests. On the other hand, strictly academic training by the same teacher who conducted the perceptual training failed to produce significant gains in either academic performance or on psychological measures. From the theoretical position maintained in this book, the perceptual training is seen as the means whereby the internal structure of the experimental group was enhanced; the improved structure thus enabled these boys to deal more effectively with the demands of the academic task. From the same theoretical position, the failure of the academic training is seen as a failure to attack the problem at its roots.

THE CURRICULUM AS A SOURCE OF PERCEPTUAL TRAINING

Certain types of curriculum activities can be modified by the teacher to promote or provide perceptual training. The chapters

---

[2]Reprinted with permission of Rosa A. Hagin and the International Reading Association.

which follow are, in effect, examples of how this can be done. The remainder of Chapter 1 will be devoted to general principles which underlie the modification of curriculum activities in order to provide perceptual training in the ongoing school experience.

The broad goal of perceptual training is to help the child structure himself and structure the space-time world in which he functions. Perceptual training activities should aim at developing the motor base and promoting the perceptual-motor match. The motor base and the perceptual-motor match are developed progressively and interdependently; often the same activity is promoting both at the same time.

The motor base is developed and refined by differentiation of the body parts and their movements, and by a subsequent integration of these parts into smooth, flexible, and generalized movement patterns. In general, differentiation develops as a child becomes aware of each part of his body as separate and distinct from the whole body, and as he learns the movements which each part is capable of making. In promoting differentiation, the teacher plans activities to help a child become aware of the individual parts of his body, and to help him move a single part without setting off excessive movements of other parts. Activities should be planned in light of the proper sequences of differentiation. Integration involves organizing the separate parts into flexible movement patterns where the parts work together. Integration develops as the child experiments with the almost unlimited possibilities for using the different parts in combination. To promote integration, the teacher plans a wide variety of activities so that as many parts as possible are brought into play. Further, any one activity should be performed in many different ways so that generalized movement patterns may develop instead of splinter skills.

The perceptual-motor match involves receiving incoming information from eyes, ears, and muscles, and organizing this information by referring it to the motor base. Through countless matchings of "outside" information to "inside" structure, the child comes, in time, to organize his world. To promote perceptual-motor matching, curriculum modifications should call for learning tasks where eyes, ears, and muscles all work together, and where information received through one sensory avenue is reinforced and verified by matching it to the motor base. Stated another way, the perceptual-motor match enables a child to experience the learning task with his body; at the perceptual-motor level the child is still learning from concrete experience. Perceptual-motor match-

The Problem and an Approach

ing is thus seen as a remedial activity for children who failed to develop the ability to structure information from their environment.

From the chapters which follow, one example may illustrate curriculum modifications which provide activities to develop the motor base and to promote the perceptual-motor match. In Chapter 2, one suggested project is the construction of a large globe map of the earth. The globe is a 3-foot diameter sphere, mounted on a suitable base, and so made as to have a fairly rough surface. The activity calls for the children to construct the globe and to draw in the lines of latitude and longitude as well as the outlines of the major land masses. Assume that the globe itself has been constructed, and that a child is now drawing the appropriate lines on the globe. The following discussion will indicate how the activity of drawing the lines contributes to the two-fold purpose of developing the motor base and promoting the perceptual-motor match.

Consider first the development of the motor base. The large size of the globe is all-important. As the child works at the top of the globe, he must assume one position for drawing; as he works at the bottom of the globe (or even at the midportion) he must assume a radically different position. Each different position demands that he utilize a separate and distinct set of muscles; however, with each different set of muscles he accomplishes the same basic task of drawing lines. By using different muscles at different times to accomplish the common goal of drawing, the child is building his motor base by developing generalized movement patterns. Here is an example of curriculum modification enhancing the development of the motor base. In addition, as the child draws on the large globe, he is learning to differentiate the parts of his body through clues provided by certain aspects of the task itself.

An activity to promote differentiation of body parts should be designed to provide a variety of simultaneous clues to the location and movements of the body parts. The activity of drawing lines on the globe is structured to provide for drawing on a rough surface with a charcoal pencil. As the child performs this task, the design of the task is such that clues to the activity of his hand are magnified. The charcoal pencil on the rough surface makes a louder sound than usual; this sound is a clue to the movement and momentary location of the hand. The charcoal pencil moving over the rough surface of the globe also produces a characteristic and magnified "feel" (or tactual-kinesthetic feedback); this "feel" is another clue to the movement and momentary location of the hand. Finally, the charcoal pencil produces a fairly broad line as it moves over the globe surface; this line is a magnified visual clue to the movement and momentary location of the hand. Thus, it can be seen that in drawing a line with a charcoal pencil on the rough surface of the globe, the child is receiving magnified clues to the movement and momentary location of his hand, and he is receiving these magnified clues simultaneously through his visual, auditory, and tactual-kinesthetic sensory avenues. Each clue helps him differentiate the hand and arm movements which produced that clue, to distinguish these parts and their movements as separate and distinct from other body parts and their movements. By such curriculum modifications, the differentiation of body parts and their movements is promoted and improved.

In addition to promoting development of generalized movement patterns and differentiation of body parts, the activity of drawing on the rough globe surface with a charcoal pencil is promoting the development of the perceptual-motor match. The stimuli which produce the visual, auditory, and tactual-kinesthetic clues to hand and arm movements all originate from the outside world. The clues to these movements all come from the environment and they all come through the appropriate sensory channels. All the clues bring information about what is going on in the outside world. As these clues come in and are matched to the motor base, the outside world progressively takes on more structure. So it can be seen that this same curriculum modification not only helps develop the motor base; it also helps the child organize his environment.

Of course, not all curriculum modifications will contribute to all the basic tasks of developing generalized movement patterns, developing differentiation, and promoting the perceptual-motor match. Some modifications will promote one or more of these aspects, while others will represent a combination. Furthermore, it should be noted that function may overlap; to some extent no one aspect functions in complete isolation from the others. A particular curriculum activity, however, may be designed to emphasize one aspect (such as differentiation) apart from the other two.

In these activities, development of the motor base and the perceptual-motor match is given practical assistance. As differentiation and integration develop more fully, the child builds a more adequate internal structure. Through the perceptual-motor match, the world of space and time comes to have a better structure. Since information from the environment comes through

The Problem and an Approach

visual, auditory, and tactual-kinesthetic channels, these channels also take on more structure and become more interrelated. In this way, perceptual training assists the child in his struggle to become a structured self functioning more adequately in a structured world.

Finally, the use of the curriculum as a tool for perceptual training must be set in larger perspective. It should be emphasized strongly that perceptual training in the curriculum is not seen as replacing perceptual training which might not be related to curriculum activities. In general, the proposals in this book are presented more as a supplement to, rather than a replacement of, a sound program of perceptual training which is aimed at remedying the child's fundamental perceptual problems. Any program of perceptual training ideally should be planned after careful diagnosis has determined the particular perceptual deficits of the individual child. Once this diagnosis has been made, the perceptual training program will consist of a number of specific activities. The main thrust of this book is to suggest ways in which the ongoing curriculum may be modified to produce some of these specific activities which a sound diagnosis might indicate as being helpful. With experience, the teacher may come to use creative curriculum modifications more and more as a means of providing those activities which a particular child needs for structuring himself and his world.

chapter 2

Perceptual Training with Social Studies

This chapter will present a specific example of perceptual training designed to accompany a social-studies curriculum, for use with a fifth-grade class. The whole project ideally should be carried out mainly by the "lower group," the "under-achievers" or "slow learners." What is presented is not a unit of study, but a project which should be considered as enrichment for the slow learners. The classroom is assumed to be a normal one engaged in a typical fifth-grade social-studies curriculum. All members of the class, including the slow learners, are assumed to be involved in the usual social-studies activities. The activities suggested in this chapter may be woven into the class program by using one or a combination of the following procedures:

1. If social-studies projects are assigned by groups, assign the project in this chapter to the slow learners.
2. Substitute the project for regular activities which may be beyond the capabilities of the slow learners.
3. Assign the project to the entire class, but give special attention to parceling out perceptual training activities to the slow learners.

In a typical fifth-grade social-studies program, the children are soon involved with history and geography. They are learning about things that happen in many different places and in many different times. The events they are studying take place thousands of miles from each other, and are also separated from the learner and from each other by centuries of time. To further complicate matters, children must move vicariously over great spans of time and space without moving themselves and without experiencing the flow of time. At one moment in class they may be "doing arithmetic," and a few moments later they are centuries away, sailing the high seas with Columbus. Within the social-studies curriculum itself, they often cover thousands of miles and many years in the same day. If their learning is to have meaning, the events, the time, and the space must all hold together.

The learning problem, then, is a complicated one, involving a high degree of structure or organization. Each event must be related to the individual child and his momentary location in time and space, and each event must be placed in its proper relation to a host of other events. If adequate structuring does not take place, some events will be jumbled together, some will not even exist for the learner, and some may float around vaguely. Solving the structure problem is quite a task for all children; for the slow learner the task is almost insurmountable. As previously noted, many slow learners are, themselves, not structured. They do not have that internal awareness which lets them know where they are in time and space; they have not established their own bodies as a zero point from which events and objects in our space-time world can be located reliably.

The project will aim at these broad goals:

1. Using the social-studies subject matter to provide visual, tactual, auditory, and kinesthetic experiences for slow learners, in such a way that these experiences will take place concurrently with the academic learning. The goal is to involve the eyes, ears, hands, muscles, and the whole body in the learning process. In this area, the project is deliberately designed to provide remediation for the slow learner while offering him academic training.

2. Using the social-studies subject matter to structure the space-time world and to relate the learner to that world. The social-studies curricula by their very nature offer rich and unique possibilities for unfolding for the child the world about him and helping him place himself in that world.

Perceptual Training with Social Studies 35

3. Motivating the slow learner by means of experiences which will give him a feeling of success. The project involves construction, mainly by the slow learners, of several items. These items, when constructed, can be used as learning aids for the whole class. Success experiences for slow learners could consist of letting them be the ones to demonstrate the items to the rest of the class. Other success experiences for slow learners will come from the actual construction of the items.

This project is presented as *one approach* to integrating perceptual training with academic subject matter. It is presented as *a solution* rather than *the solution*. It is meant to be an example of how integration can be achieved rather than a prescription. Hopefully, it will be suggestive rather than definitive. The perceptive teacher can accomplish the goals by developing a wide variety of quite different projects. Those who use this project are encouraged to make their own creative variations.

THE PROJECT: AN OVERVIEW

Basically, the project consists of constructing and using a globe map, a floor map, and a time line, all three items made on a very large scale. These items are basic ingredients of a fifth-grade social-studies curriculum, and are used as learning tools with nearly all social studies. The project, therefore, will not be confined to a particular unit, but will be used with all those social-studies units where events are to be located in time and place.

The project should be started as soon as practicable after the class begins social studies, at least as soon as times and places are encountered. Since the construction phase will involve the use of some basic mathematical concepts, the slow learners might begin on the project during time allotted to arithmetic. Much of the project, and especially the construction phase, will be of real help to those slow learners whose difficulties with mathematics are related to poor concepts of objects in space.

The project is designed so that perceptual training will be provided both while the items are being made and while they are being used as aids for classroom study. Perceptual training will come naturally as the children go through the project; however, this training can be increased greatly if the teacher will take advantage of spontaneous situations which inevitably will arise. It is impossible to point out all the training opportunities in a project such as this, but the teacher can see them as the project unfolds. The project description, therefore, will indicate the major aspects of perceptual training offered, realizing that the teacher will add many elements on his own initiative.

The perceptual training offered by each major element of the project is presented in outline form below.

I. *Construction Phase*
    A. Constructing the Globe Map
       1. Making styrofoam rings (which will be formed into the sphere).
          a. *Perceptual-motor Matching:* Sawing concentric rings from styrofoam gives simultaneous visual, auditory, and tactual-kinesthetic feedback.
          b. *Differentiation:* Feedback promotes awareness of parts used in the task.
          c. *Integration:* Coordinated movements are developed. Control of movement is developed.
          d. *Generalization:* Different sizes of rings are made, thus varying the movements involved.
       2. Assembling styrofoam rings into outline of sphere.
          Form Perception: Parts are assembled into a whole. Motor and visual activity are both involved; the child *experiences* the whole coming together from the parts.
       3. Making the globe surface with papier-maché clay.
          a. *Perceptual-motor Matching:* Visual and tactual-kinesthetic feedback comes from hands spreading clay.
          b. *Differentiation:* Clay gives unique tactual-kinesthetic feedback which promotes awareness of those parts involved in the task.
          c. *Integration:* Two hands and arms work together in spreading clay; coordination and control are developed.
          d. *Generalization:* Working on top, bottom, and sides requires different body positions and much variety of muscle combinations to do the same task.
       4. Locating North and South Poles.
          a. *Directionality, Spatial Relations:* North Pole is located by children observing (from a distance)

and pointing to high point on globe; motor is involved with visual in indicating relations.
b. *Generalization:* South Pole location involves same task, but radically different body positions and movements.
5. Locating and drawing equator, lines of longitude and latitude, and outlines of land masses.
a. *Perceptual-motor Matching:* Globe surface is rough sand finish; drawing is done with charcoal pencil. Drawing thus provides visual, auditory, and tactual-kinesthetic feedback.
b. *Differentiation:* See preceding sections on differentiation.
c. *Integration:* See preceding sections on integration.
d. *Generalization:* Task requires variety of body movements and muscle combinations.
e. *Form Perception:* Whole is *experienced* from visual, auditory, and tactual-kinesthetic involvement of child with parts.

B. Constructing the Time Line.

The construction phase for the time line provides relatively little perceptual training. The children will divide a very long line into centuries and decades, and will thus experience a whole being broken down into parts. The "Use Phase" will offer considerably more perceptual training (see below).

C. Constructing the Floor Map.
1. Tracing over a large United States map which is projected onto a 9 x 13 foot plastic sheet. The plastic sheet is placed on a wall, and the map is projected with an opaque projector; children trace map with charcoal pencils.
a. *Perceptual-motor Matching:* See preceding sections.
b. *Differentiation:* See preceding sections.
c. *Integration:* See preceding sections.
d. *Generalization:* Large size of map involves many different body positions and muscle combinations. Projection of trace offers opportunity to work with midline problems.
e. *Form Perception:* Whole is first perceived visually; then parts are experienced through all major sensory-motor avenues. Finished product

is a whole from experienced parts.
2. Inking over pencil lines (map on floor; use felt-tip pens).
   a. *Generalization:* Entirely different body positions and muscle combinations. Work previously done in vertical plane is now done in horizontal plane.
   b. *Perceptual-motor matching, differentiation, integration,* and *form perception* are promoted also.
3. Orienting the Map.

   Orienting marks are placed on the floor and map, so that "map North" may be oriented readily with "ground North." Training in spatial relations and directions results. This learning utilizes motor activity along with visual. Directions and relations are thus experienced motorically as well as visually.

Use Phase
A. Using the Globe Map.

   Once constructed, globe map may be used as would any other. Size, rough surface, and initial absence of national boundaries make possible the following major types of perceptual training:
   1. *Relations among objects in space:* Graphic demonstrations of objects moving over horizon are possible because of size. Large size also makes possible concrete demonstration of latitude determination.
   2. *Spatial and temporal orientations:* National and state boundaries are drawn as events involving map locations are studied; children are helped to correlate events in time with map locations. Sensory-motor activity in drawing thus adds additional dimensions to associating temporal events with spatial locations of those events.
   3. *Perceptual-motor matching and form perception:* Rough surfaces of globe may be exploited in many ways. Example: children trace outlines of continents, routes of explorers, and the like with fingers moving over rough surface.
B. Using the Time Line.

   Time line is quite long (20 to 30 feet) and divided into centuries and decades. Children hang cards listing events studied at proper time locations on line. All events studied to date are placed on line *each day*, and removed at end of day. Major perceptual training:

Temporal-spatial relations: Time is translated into a visible scale located in space: the time line. Visual-motor activity is required to place a card indicating an event in time; thus time unfolds and is organized (relatively) in terms of the activity involved in hanging a card at a particular place. Further, the time line represents a chronological outline of social-studies activities to date. Each day the child experiences an expanding block of time he has given to social studies; he experiences this in terms of his visual perception of the time line and the cards on it and by the visual-motor experience of building the block of time anew each day. Training is also given in form perception as locations are determined in relation to location of events on the line.

C. Using the Floor Map.

Large map size is the key to perceptual training with the floor map. Major perceptual training is in *spatial relations*. Locations of events studied may be experienced in terms of motor activity in moving from one place to another on the large map.

The main emphasis in the foregoing outline has been to suggest how perceptual training results from project activities. The project activities themselves will be presented now in more complete form. The outline may be consulted whenever project activities need relating to perceptual training goals. Many variations of activities may be planned to add additional training.

CONSTRUCTION PHASE

a. Constructing the Globe Map

The globe itself should be approximately 3 feet in diameter. If it is made much smaller than 30 inches its effectiveness will be decreased. Two different methods for making the globe are suggested. The method described in this section is easy; a harder method is described in the Appendix.

Before presenting the easy method, let a word be said in behalf of the harder one. It offers many more opportunities for perceptual training. It will not add to the academic aspects of social studies, but it should certainly be remedial for arithmetic. If the time can be made available, the harder method will more than repay the extra effort required. Briefly, this method consists of using sheets of styrofoam 1 inch thick, cutting progressively smaller rings from these sheets, and stacking the rings on top of each other to form a rough hemisphere; the process is repeated for the second hemisphere, and the rings are glued together. The surface is made smooth by filling in the gaps at the outer edges of the rings with a suitable filler. Figure A-1 in the Appendix illustrates the construction procedure. Cutting the rings gives a wealth of experience in matching visual data to tactual, kinesthetic, and auditory data. The cutting instrument is a bare hacksaw blade; styrofoam is so easy to cut that no handle is needed for the blade. A child can cut the material quickly and easily, and with very brief instructions can attain competence. The writer has seen a first-grader cut a 36-inch circle with more than acceptable accuracy and with no previous experience.

The easy method is to obtain a large plastic beach ball, the kind which is made with segments of plastic bonded together leaving only very fine seams when inflated. Inflate the ball and paint it with two coats of latex base paint; the first coat is applied as it comes from the can, but a "sand float finish" material (obtainable at paint stores) is added to the paint before the second coat is applied. The finished surface is identical to the "plastered" finish put on interior wallboard in homes, and gives the rough texture needed.

The following additional construction details apply to the globe map regardless of whether the sphere is made by the hard or by the easy method.

After the globe itself has been made, the next step is to add the lines of longitude and latitude. Explain to the group what these lines are, and how they are used to locate any position on the earth. A regular classroom globe should be used for this explanation. Since the regular classroom globe will be used frequently as a model during construction, it would be well to obtain one which has the lines of longitude and latitude marked quite clearly. Tell the group they will put these lines on the globe, and that the first task is to locate the North Pole.

Explain that the North Pole will be at the top of the globe; they must find the highest place on the globe. (Ignore the tilt of the earth to simplify construction.) Tell them that their eyes may

Perceptual Training with Social Studies 41

fool them if they try to find the high point by looking. To demonstrate this, place four or five dots randomly in the near vicinity of the top of the globe, and ask each class member to indicate which one he thinks is the top or closest to the top. A difference of opinion probably will arise. The random dots should then be removed.

To locate the North Pole accurately, use a team of three children. One child stands by the globe and holds a pencil touching the approximate location of the pole; a second child stands several steps away from the globe and facing it; the third child also stands several steps away from and facing the globe, but at right angles to the other two and in such a position that the pencil forms the vertex of a right angle (see Figure 2-1). The child holding the pencil moves the pencil either right or left as each child tells him. He first takes directions from one child, moving the pencil either right or left, until the point of the pencil is on the topmost point of the globe *as that child sees it*. Then, without moving the pencil, he turns to the other child, and moves the pencil right or left *as the other child sees it*. He repeats this process, taking directions

FIGURE 2-1.   Locating the North Pole

from first one child and then the other, until both see the pencil point at the very top without further moves. This point is the North Pole, and should be marked plainly. To increase accuracy, go through the entire procedure several times, using different children. Several dots quite close together should be obtained, and the final location of the pole should be made in the center of the group of dots.

The South Pole should be located in the same manner, but the team of three children should lie on the floor. To turn the globe upside down would, of course, be easier, but lying on the floor will add to the variety of positions and encourage more generalized movements.

The next step is to locate the equator. Remind the group that the equator is halfway between the North and South Poles, and show them on the classroom globe how it goes around the earth like a belt. Tell them they should start by finding just one point which is halfway between the two poles, and ask if anyone can think how to find the point that is exactly in the middle. If they have trouble responding (and they probably will), show them a piece of stout string about 6 feet long, and ask, "Can you use this?" If they still have trouble, have one child hold the string on the North Pole while another stretches it down to the South Pole. Have them fold the measured length in half, and tie a short piece of string at the midpoint. One end can then be placed on the North Pole and stretched to the midpoint, and a mark can be made which is one point on the equator.

Now point out that the North Pole is at the *highest* part of the globe and that the equator goes around the *widest* part. Suggest that they could have used the wall to find the widest part, and they would not have had to use the string. Ask if anyone knows how to use the wall to find the widest part. If they have trouble with this question, ask one of them to move the globe close to a smooth section of vertical wall. Have them look at the globe and the wall, and ask if they can now see how the wall shows which part is the widest. Then have them move the globe until it barely touches the wall, and mark the contact point on the globe (see Figure 2-2). This point is on the equator. Next, have them find the point which they measured with the string, and turn the globe so that this point faces the wall. Have them move the globe until it again just touches the wall, and mark the contact point on the globe. The two marks (one from string measure and one from wall contact) should be quite close to the same height from the floor.

Perceptual Training with Social Studies 43

FIGURE 2-2. **Locating the Equator**

While the globe is at the wall it will be convenient to mark a number of points so that the equator can be drawn by connecting these points. The globe is placed against the wall (barely touching), a mark is made on the globe, the globe is then shifted and again placed against the wall and marked; this process is continued until a series of marks outlines the equator. The children can then draw in the equator by connecting the marks. All drawing and marking should be done with soft-lead pencil or charcoal pencil at this point. When the entire globe map is finished, the pencil lines can be gone over with felt-tip pens or some other suitable instrument.

Now the North and South Poles and the equator are located on the globe. The next step is to add the lines of latitude and longitude. It is important that the constructed globe have the same divisions between the marked lines as does the classroom globe. The children will use the classroom globe as a guide to mark off the outlines of the major land masses, and if the lines of latitude and longitude are marked off in different units the children will become confused when they come to this stage. So have the group examine the classroom globe carefully. They should count the number of latitude "spaces" around the whole globe. Explain that they will divide the globe they make into the same number of "spaces," and will number the spaces in the same way as they are on the regular globe.

Latitude lines will probably be drawn on the globe for each 10 degrees. Nine equal divisions must be made from the equator to the North Pole, making a total of 90 degrees in this arc. Have someone run a string from the North Pole straight down to the equator, and mark this distance on the string. The problem is to divide this distance into nine equal parts. Measuring and dividing by use of arithmetic will most likely result in unwieldy fractions. A simpler way is to draw on the chalkboard parallel lines 2 inches apart, marking off nine spaces 2 inches wide (the teacher should do this). Then stretch the measured length of string at an angle across the lines until each end of the string is on one of the outside lines. Mark the string where each line crosses it, and the string is divided into nine equal parts (see Figure 2-3).

FIGURE 2-3.   Using Parallel Lines to Divide a String into Equal Parts

Perceptual Training with Social Studies 45

Have the children take the divided string and place one end on the North Pole and run the other end straight down to the equator. Two children should hold the string in position while a third makes a mark on the globe opposite each mark on the string. Then lift the end lying on the equator until that end is at least as high as the end on the pole, and shift the string slightly to one side and again run it straight down to the equator. Now another set of latitude divisions can be marked on the globe opposite each mark on the string (see Figure 2-4). Repeat this until the string has been worked all around the globe. Repeat the process for the South Pole, removing the globe from its base if necessary. Put the globe back on the base and have the children draw in the lines of latitude by connecting the marks. The children should take turns working the string and marking, and as many as possible should be at work at the same time drawing in the latitude lines. In parceling out the work, try to see that each child does some work on the top, middle, and bottom of the globe. Do not permit turning the globe to make the drawing more convenient; the drawing should be done from different and unusual body positions.

To lay out the lines of longitude, begin by making an arbitrary mark at any point on the equator, and label this point "0." Place one end of a long piece of string on the point and run the string

FIGURE 2-4.   **Marking Points for Lines of Latitude**

all around the globe, keeping the string on the equator. Several children will be needed to keep the string in place. When the circumference of the globe has been measured with the string, remove the string and fold it in half, marking the midpoint. Place the end of the string on the "0" mark again, and this time run it around the equator only halfway. Place a mark on the equator at the midpoint of the string, and label this point "180." In similar fashion, locate 90-degree (east and west) points on the equator, and label them. The equator is now divided into four equal quandrants. If the classroom globe is divided into 10-degree intervals of longitude, then each 90-degree quandrant will be divided into nine equal parts. If the intervals are 15 degrees, then the quandrants will have six equal divisions. When these divisions have been marked on the equator, a line of longitude may be located by running a string from the North Pole through a division mark on the equator and on down to the South Pole (see Figure 2-5). The string should be kept straight, and the longitude line may be marked by using the string as a guide. The children, of course, should do all the measuring, marking, and drawing of lines.

The globe now has both poles and the lines of latitude and longitude drawn in with pencil or charcoal. Before outlining the

FIGURE 2-5.   Drawing Lines of Longitude with String Guide

land masses, it would be well to go over the light lines with a brightly colored felt pen or other instrument to make the lines stand out. Also, at this time the lines should be labeled, using the classroom globe as a guide.

Take time to explain the major features of latitude and longitude to the group while only these lines are on the globe. Show them how these lines are used to locate a position on the map. Write several positions on the board, giving latitude and longitude of each position, and have the children point to the position on the globe. Spend as much time as necessary so that everyone in the group is able to handle these relationships. The procedure can be varied and enriched by having the children locate a certain city on the classroom globe, determine its latitude and longitude, and then locate it on the globe they have made.

Interpolating within a section of the globe marked off by lines of latitude and longitude will represent a real step forward for many slow learners. For example, if they can learn to visualize 24 degrees latitude as "not quite halfway between 20 and 30 degrees," and can make such estimates consistently, they will have made a significant gain. Those who cannot do this by visual inspection should use a finger or stylus to trace the distances from one division to another, repeating this until they get the "feel" of the distance. They can then practice moving one-half, one-third, one-fourth of the distance; they can do this for different parts of the globe, which will involve doing it from different body, arm, and hand positions. The tactual-kinesthetic experience will have additional reinforcement if the child will say aloud "one-half" or "one-fourth" as he moves the corresponding distance.

The next step is to have the children draw in the land areas on the globe, using the regular classroom globe as a model. Each child should be assigned a major area so that he has a complete figure to deal with. One could draw North America, another South America, another Africa, and so on. In this phase, form perception can be trained: First the child should experience his assigned area as a whole figure. Then he should experience the various elements of that figure as he reproduces it on a larger scale. Finally he should experience the whole figure coming together from its elements. In effect he will be getting a whole figure, breaking it up into smaller elements which will be easier for him to handle, and then reassembling the whole from the elements. By having him do this on a different scale, generalization has been added.

The following procedure should help the child do this task: Use the regular classroom globe to assign the child his area. Have him trace the outline with his finger. Ask him to look at the globe and pick out the lines of latitude and longitude which are just outside the total figure, and which form a rough boundary for his whole area (see Figure 2-6). Have him write down his boun-

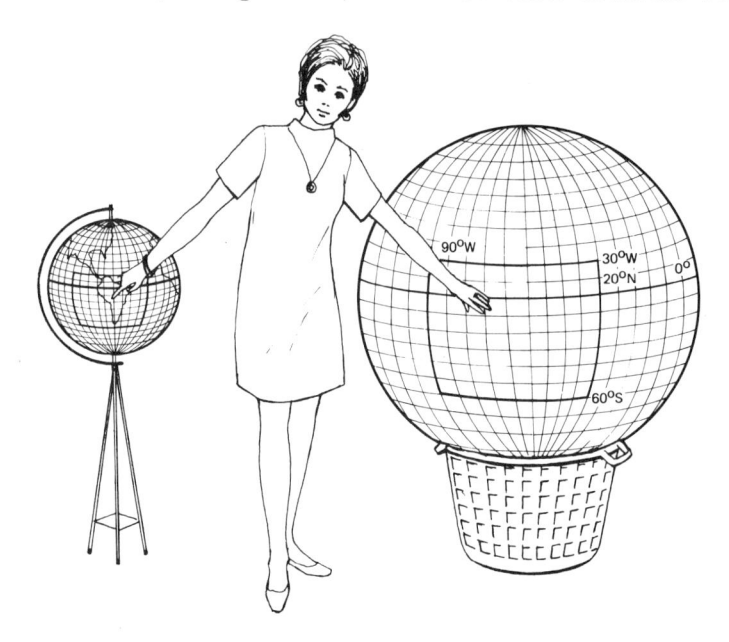

FIGURE 2-6.   **An Assigned Area Marked Off for One Child**

daries in some such fashion as this: "South America is between latitude 20 degrees north and latitude 60 degrees south. It is also between longitude 30 degrees west and longitude 90 degrees west." Now have him locate these same "boundaries" on the globe being constructed, and mark in charcoal along each boundary so that he can readily identify the rough area in which he will be working. By now, he should have the whole figure fairly well in mind, and he should be aware of its relative location with respect to the globe.

To divide the whole figure into more manageable parts, take advantage of the crisscrossing lines of longitude and latitude. Ask the child to point out on the regular globe the place where he would like to start his drawing. When he has done this, show him that his starting point is inside a small figure of four sides made up of longitude and latitude lines (see Figure 2-7). Then go to

Perceptual Training with Social Studies 49

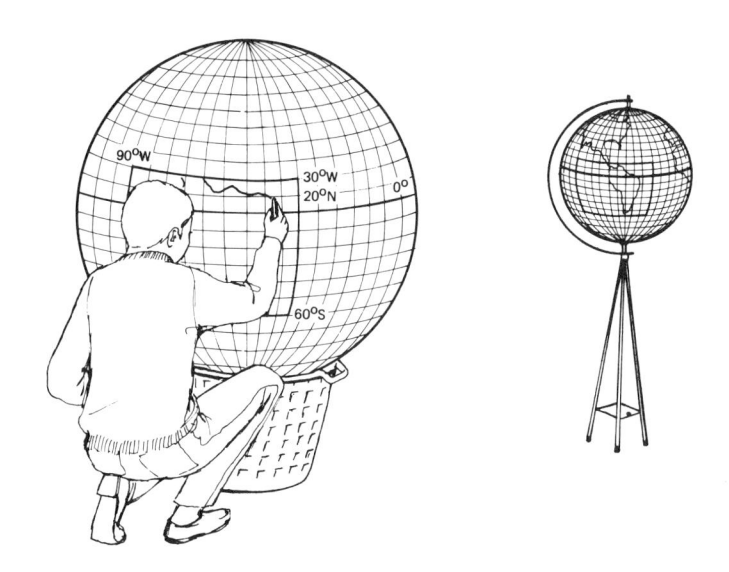

FIGURE 2-7. **Drawing the Assigned Area in Segments**

the other globe, locate the same small segment of the globe, and have him mark where he will start his drawing. Now go back to the regular globe, and point out how every part of the outline is in one of these small segments of the globe. Ask him to draw his outline one part at a time, but to draw each part as it follows the one before it. He should do this drawing with pencil or charcoal so that errors may be corrected. When the child has completed the drawing, he has experienced the figure as a number of parts in orderly sequence.

The whole figure can be brought together again simply by having the child trace over his own lines with a felt pen or other marker. Have him start at a different point and draw this time in the opposite direction from the one he used to outline his area. Do not let him follow the "segmenting" by which he originally produced the figure; he should draw with a much freer and more sweeping movement now.

The globe map is now virtually complete, except for any refinements the teacher may wish to make, such as coloring the oceans and lakes and labeling the continents. Borders of nations and states should not be added until such times as these places are studied; they can be added one at a time as they are encountered.

b. Constructing the Time Line

The time line can be made in a variety of ways, depending upon the arrangement of the classroom and the teacher's preference. It consists only of some form of a straight line divided into centuries and decades, arranged so that labels can be added and removed easily. What is recommended is the usual time line made larger and more flexible. It should be nearly as long as the classroom (at least 20 feet long). It could turn a corner if necessary to obtain the desired length.

The time line should be laid out on a scale of ¼ inch to 1 year. A line 20 feet long would therefore represent a span of time of some 960 years, which would embrace the times of the Viking explorers to the present. If the teacher does not intend to deal with this large a time span during the school year, the scale could be made ½ inch to 1 year. In this case a 30-foot line would cover 720 years or a 20-foot line would cover 480 years. Basically, a long line is suggested which will represent the total span of time studied during the school year.

The line itself could be a length of stout cord stretched taut along a wall, along the top of the chalkboard, under the chalk tray, or even in the middle of the room; any convenient place will do. It should be parallel to the floor, and its height should be such that a child must reach, stoop, or squat (or get into some other unusual position) in order to touch the line. If a small ladder or sturdy chair is available it would be well to have the line high enough that one of these would be needed in order for a child to get to the line. The slow learners will be using the line frequently, and it should be necessary for them to assume unusual positions as they do so. In planning for this aspect, safety should be underscored, especially since some slow learners have unusual and often unnoticed problems in balance, coordination, and vision.

The line may also be made of a strip of masking tape running along a wall, or a background of butcher's paper running along a wall with a narrower strip of paper or tape fastened to this background. Whatever type line is used, provision should be made for attaching and removing all labels. Clothespins, paper clips, and similar fasteners will work well with labels on a cord, but if a tape line on a wall is used, then some other means of fastening must be provided.

After selecting the size, type, and scale of the line, have the children divide the line by measuring with a ruler. This work could best be done by working at a table and measuring the line before it is installed in its permanent location. The children should first measure off the centuries (25 inches is one century if the ¼-inch scale is used). If the line is made of cord, the divisions could be marked by tying a short piece of colored string or yarn around the cord at the proper place. After the centuries have been marked, each century should be divided into 10-year intervals. These decades should be marked with a different color string. Labels should then be made on cards (at least size 5 x 7) for each century and each half century (1500, 1550, 1600, and so on). The century labels should be written in one color and the half-century labels should be in another color.

When all the labels have been made, let the children stretch the string (or put up any other kind of line which may have been selected), and attach each label at its proper place. Explain that the line represents time, and that they have divided the time into centuries and decades. After the children have inspected the finished product, remove the labels and put them away for future use. A supply of blank labels should be obtained; this completes the equipment needed for use of the line. The blank labels will be used for writing in events as they are studied, and these should be larger than the time labels. All labels should be of sturdy stock which will not curl unduly when the labels are suspended.

c. Constructing the Floor Map

The floor map of the United States should be made quite large; large enough, in fact that a child in walking on it would experience a noticeable amount of movement as he crosses several states. If possible, it should be as large as 9 x 13 feet; every effort should be made to have it no smaller than 6 x 9 feet. These dimensions are suggested because they are roughly proportional to the length and breadth of the nation, and also because the recommended materials can be used in their standard width with only one seam. If these dimensions seem to make excessive demands upon classroom floor space, remember that the map need be on the floor only while it is being used; at other times it can be folded or rolled into a small bundle for storage.

The recommended material is plastic upholstery material, available in the dime store in widths of 54 inches (4½ feet). Two widths can therefore be joined to make a 9-foot dimension. One side has a pattern, but the other side is plain; the map should be constructed on the plain side. To make the map "sheet" in the 9 x 13 size, obtain two pieces of the material, each piece being 13 feet long, and join them together with a strip of 3-inch surgical tape or masking tape. The tape should be applied on the reverse side of the map, which would be the patterned side of the material. The 6 x 9 size can be made the same way, except that in this case each of the two pieces need be only 6 feet long. This material is inexpensive and quite tough, and will take much rough wear from walking, turning, shifting position, as well as from folding and rolling.

An overhead opaque projector should be used to project a map of the United States onto the large map sheet, and the children should trace over the projected lines with charcoal pencils. The opaque projector is the type which will project from a printed page; however, if a transparency map is available, the overhead transparent projector will do as well. For this part of the construction, the large plastic map sheet should be tacked temporarily to a wall. The projector should be at right angles to and centered on the sheet to avoid distortion, and the projected image should be as large as the sheet will allow. With the image on the sheet, have the children trace the outline of the United States and the boundaries of the individual states (omitting Alaska and Hawaii unless the teacher wishes to add them as an "inset"). The map obtained for this purpose should be clear, and the lines of latitude and longitude need to be marked on it in 5-degree intervals. In selecting the map, see that the latitude and longitude lines are printed across the map itself (on some maps these lines stop at the boundaries), and have the children trace these lines as well as the boundaries. Number each line of latitude and longitude.

Several children can trace at the same time. Note that in tracing they will be working in many different body positions as they attack the lower and upper portions of the projected map. This variety of body positions is highly desirable. Furthermore, the children must trace from beside the line they are working on at a given moment, or else their bodies will cast a shadow and obscure the projected pattern. This problem will necessitate still more variation of body movement. You will probably find that right-handed children will tend to stand to the left of the spot they are working on, while left-handed children will stand to the right. If a child does this consistently he is probably avoiding crossing his vertical midline; in such a case he should be corrected

Perceptual Training with Social Studies 53

and required to alternate so that his hand will work across the midline as well as on the side of the working hand. The upper portions of the map will be out of reach of the children, and short ladders or other safe standings will be needed. To avoid requiring the children to work from undue heights, try taping a charcoal pencil to a pointer for extra "reach," for this will add to the training considerably, and at the same time will solve a practical problem.

When the tracing is completed, put the map on the floor and have the children go over the traced lines with a felt-tip pen. The national boundaries should be in a dark color and the state boundaries should be made very pale. Explain to the children that we did not always have the same states, and that boundaries changed from time to time. Tell them that they will trace in the state lines in darker colors when they study about them.

Let the children locate their school on the map, using road maps to compare with the floor map. Mark and label this location, and draw a North line from their school location all the way to the north edge of the sheet, making this line parallel to the longitude lines, and using the longitude lines as a guide. Then place the map in the location where it will be used, and let the North line on the map point roughly to north. Have one child stand on the map at the point where the school location was marked, and determine as accurately as possible which direction is north from this point. When this has been determined, shift the map until the North line is actually pointing north. Without moving the map, extend the line from the school location south until the line is at the south edge of the sheet. When this extension is made, a North-South line will run through the school location, and across the entire sheet. With the map still in place, put a piece of tape on the floor in such a place that the tape is next to the north end of the line; do the same at the south end. Make a short extension of each end of the line so that the line goes off of the sheet and on to the tape. Label these short extensions "North" and "South" respectively. Move the map a short distance and show the children that they can get the map pointing north again by matching the line on the map with the two marks on the tapes.

Explain how the map is oriented whenever the North line on the map is pointing to north on the ground. Also tell them that when the map North line is pointing at north on the ground, then all the places on the map are in their "real" direction from the school location and from each other. Demonstrate this fact by having one of the children stand on the school location; then tell him, "You want to go to Texas. Show us Texas on the map. Which direction would you go if you went straight to Texas?" Have him walk to Texas on the map; then have him walk back to school. Several variations of this should be made until the children begin to experience the relative directions. Be sure that they see not only the "map directions," but also the "ground directions" as related to real directions in the classroom itself. Choose several places so that they can look out a window and visualize directions extending beyond the room itself. When everyone understands that the map directions are the same as the "real directions" on the ground, the construction phase of the floor map is then complete, and the map can be stored until needed for instruction.

II. USE PHASE

After the children have made the three items, they can use them whenever the class is studying events which happened at a given time and place. The unobtrusive selection of slow learners to work with these materials is suggested.

a. Using the Globe Map

The globe map may be used in several ways which its large size makes possible. The children can see how men began to think the earth was curved as they watched ships come over the horizon and noticed that the taller parts were sighted first and then, progressively, the lower parts. Make a sighting device about ½ inch in diameter from a rolled piece of paper, and tape it to the globe. For realism, one end could be located on the west coast of Portugal so that the "lookout" is looking west over the Atlantic Ocean. Let one child sight through the tube while another moves a piece of chalk toward him slowly, sliding the chalk vertically along the globe surface as the mast of a ship would appear (see Figure 2-8). The chalk should be started over the horizon from the lookout, and he should tell when he first sees the top of the chalk. The chalk can then be moved closer to him and stopped; he then can mark with a pencil the lowest part of the chalk which is visible to him through the tube; the chalk is then moved closer, stopped, and marked again. As a variation, other objects can be

FIGURE 2-8. Using the Globe to See an Object Over the Horizon

moved and the viewer required to sketch the parts he sees at various distances. Still another useful variation can be obtained by letting the viewer move the object himself.

Any globe can be used to demonstrate how a ship determines its longitude by knowing Greenwich Mean Time at high noon at its position. Demonstrating how latitude is determined is another matter, and is more effective if a large globe, such as the one the children made, is available. The navigator measures the angle from the horizon to the sun at high noon, and this angle is known as the altitude. The greater the angle, the smaller the latitude. To demonstrate this relationship, use a chalkboard eraser as a ship. Use a piece of string about 20 feet long, and tape the string to the eraser about 2 feet from one end, the tape being wound around the eraser several times at the "amidships" point. The short end of the string will represent the line of sight to the horizon; the longer end, the line of sight to the sun. Use three children in the demonstration: one to move the ship, one to stretch the short line to the horizon, and one to hold the long end and to represent the sun. Have the three children take their places, with the ship slightly north of the equator (Figure 2-9).

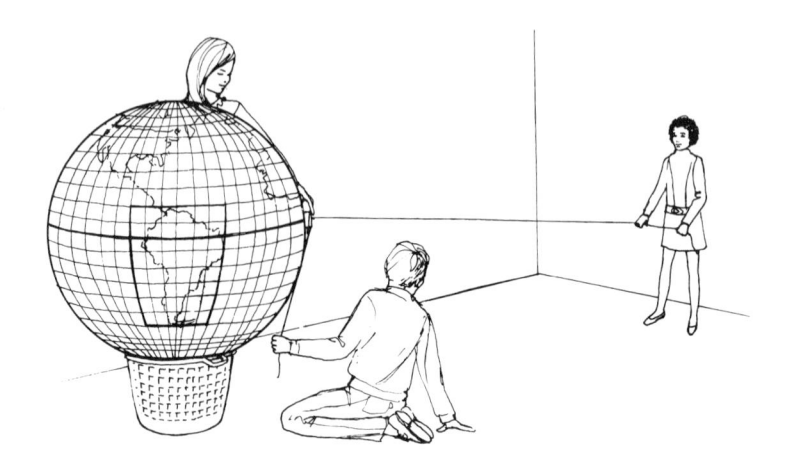

FIGURE 2-9.   **Demonstrating Latitude Relationships**

When the short line has been stretched downward until one point touches the globe, the horizon has been determined. When the long line is stretched, it represents a ray from the sun. Point out the angle between the horizon and the sun, and explain that this angle is called the altitude angle; also point out that the ship is close to the equator and that therefore its latitude is small. Then move the ship north, stop, and observe the latitude and the size of the altitude angle. The decrease in altitude angle and increase in latitude should be noticeable. This demonstration is not completely accurate, because the sun's rays are parallel. The teacher may not want to add this refinement lest the children become confused with too much technical data. Should the teacher wish to add the refinement, the child representing the sun must keep the long line parallel to the floor at all times.

b. Using the Time Line

The time line may be used in this manner: Each session should start with the line bare of all labels; even the labels for the centuries and half centuries should have been removed at the close of the previous day. Assume the class is studying the signing of the Declaration of Independence. As the session starts, one child should put the century and half-century markers up, so that all

Perceptual Training with Social Studies 57

the time to be covered during the whole school year is marked out anew for each session. Then another child should put up the labels of all the events studied before the present session on the Declaration of Independence. One label with a color different from all the rest and bearing a legend such as "Today we are here" is placed on the time line at "1776." Some time during the session, one child should make a new label proclaiming "1776—Declaration of Independence signed" and any other information the teacher wishes. Toward the close of the session, the "Today we are here" label is replaced by the newly-made label. By the end of the school day all labels should be removed and stored for use at the next session.

In using the time line in this fashion, the teacher is providing many different opportunities for movements to be associated with points in time, the flow of time, and the fact that events occur in a time dimension where there is a "before" and an "after" and a "during." Only centuries and half-centuries are labeled, and decades are marked but not labeled; therefore, each time a label is put at a point on the line, it involves coping with a space measurement as well as a time location. To locate 1776, a child must find 1750 (which is labeled), count off two more decades beyond this, estimate six-tenths of the distance into the third decade, and put the label at this point. To put up different labels at different times, he must move over significant distances because of the scale of the line. As he puts the century and half-century markers in place (they should be put up in chronological order), his perception of the flow of time should be aided by his movements from 1400 to 1450 to 1500, for example. The time line permits adding body movements and manipulations of labels on a line to the visual and auditory experience of reading and hearing about events.

c. Using the Floor Map

As an example of class use of the floor map, assume the same learning situation about the signing of the Declaration of Independence. It soon will be established that this happened in Philadelphia on July 4, 1776. A child should be asked to locate Philadelphia, first on the globe and then on the floor map. The floor map is oriented so that "north on the map" is pointing to "north on the ground." The location of the school is a permanent fixture of the floor map, so another child should be asked to stand on the map at the school location, and from this point show where Philadelphia is on the map. He should then walk on the map from school to Philadelphia and back to school from Philadelphia. When he is again at school, ask him to show the group the actual direction he would travel if he were going straight to Philadelphia (the "ground direction" and not just a "map direction"). Then point out the fact the direction on the map is the same as the actual direction to Philadelphia. Have another child give the name of the direction. Have others pretend that they live in different cities, and let them discover the directions from their cities to Philadelphia by actually standing on the different map locations, walking to Philadelphia, pointing out actual directions, and naming those directions.

Some slow learners have difficulty translating from a horizontal to a vertical plane; therefore, it would be well to use a wall map of the United States in conjunction with the floor map. A child may be able to handle directions on the floor map and still become confused with a wall map on which north is now "up" instead of "over there," east is "right" instead of "that way," and the like. The wall map should be used at least as long as any child is experiencing this difficulty.

CONCLUSION

Additional use of the time line and the globe and floor map, along with added perceptual training, is provided by drawing internal boundaries at the times when particular nations, states, territories, and the like are first studied in the class program. Whenever a boundary is drawn on the floor map of the United States, the same boundary should be drawn on the globe. The dates associated with new boundaries often may be identified on the time line. If construction is completed progressively by drawing boundaries as the corresponding places are studied, the two maps would provide, at any given moment, a graphic record of every place studied to date, and this record would correspond to that provided by the time line.

In addition to these specific recommended uses of the materials, it is assumed that the two maps and the time line would provide the teacher with three visual aids of a type commonly used with social-studies curricula. They could be used in the same manner as any other maps and time lines are used. The fact that the visual aids were constructed by the children should result in added enthusiasm and increased motivation.

This project weaves perceptual training in with academic training. It consists of a construction phase and a use phase. Each phase contains both academic and perceptual training. In designing the project, an attempt has been made to translate the academic structure into meaningful activities which represent perceptual training.

chapter 3

Perceptual Training with the Language Arts

This chapter will present a unit on reading for first grade, and will suggest ways of including perceptual training as an organic part of the unit.

An excellent and frequently recommended supplementary tool for teaching reading in first grade is the experience method described by Kirk (1940, pp. 80-81). Curriculum-makers use varying terms to describe the process; in this unit, the term "experience chart" will be used. In making an experience chart, the children first share some common experience such as a trip to a farm, a nature walk, or a visit to a supermarket. Later, in the classroom, the teacher and the children discuss the experience, and the teacher suggests that they write a story about the different things they did. In an informal way, the children compose short statements about what they saw and otherwise experienced, and the teacher writes these down on a large chart in the children's own words. The children read from the chart with the teacher's help. A common variation is to construct the experience chart from spontaneous or even individual experiences: a party, a holiday, a fire drill.

The experience chart is usually recommended for use during the child's earliest reading experiences (Harris, 1961, pp. 77-79). This use seems wise, for some children have difficulty connecting words on a printed page with events in their active world; how much better to have their earliest encounter with words flow from their own experience. The experience-chart approach has drawbacks, however. Vocabulary is not controlled and is not repeated sufficiently, and some children memorize the chart without learning the words. For this reason Harris (p. 79) recommends that experience charts be " . . . used as an introduction to reading and as a supplement to basal readers rather than a substitute for them. . . . " The unit presented is therefore recommended for the period of beginning reading.

THE UNIT: AN OVERVIEW

This unit proposes that the children learn to play "kickball," that they play each day until they have mastered the game and its structure, and that they compose stories about their experience. The teacher will write each story on a chart, and the children will read from the charts, using them as part of their stock of beginning reading materials. Involvement with the game itself could take place during recess and/or the time for physical education. The unit also will offer some suggestions for remediation of basic perceptual problems which probably will be noted as the children play kickball. The teacher may wish to begin some of the remediation while unit activities are still in progress; some remediation may extend past the time allotted for the unit. The recess and physical education periods can provide opportunity to help children overcome many perceptual problems.

The game of kickball is a variation of baseball. It has four bases, and players make runs as in baseball. The game is played by two sides, and each side is "up" until it makes three "outs." Instead of using a bat to start the ball in play, a player kicks the ball which is rolled toward him by the pitcher. The ball can be a volleyball or a sturdy inflated rubber or plastic ball of approximately the same size. The baseball rules for fouls, fly balls, runs, outs, and the like all apply, except that in kickball a player may be put out by being hit with the ball, in addition to the other ways he may be put out. Kickball does not require the precision necessary for baseball or softball, and the only equipment needed is a ball and four bases. The number of players can vary; two teams can be formed by dividing the first-grade class into two equal groups. Extra players can be added to the outfield.

Perceptual Training with the Language Arts

Why kickball? Mainly because children who are playing this game are getting a great deal of perceptual training in the process. A lot of sheer activity is taking place, and this activity is quite varied. Many children from all strata of society do not routinely engage in vigorous and varied activities which help develop flexible movements, body awareness, and motor coordination. Kickball and similar games can help alleviate some of these deficits, and can help that basic development which is essential for good perception.

Consider some of the activities the game involves. Children kick, run, stop and start, catch, throw, dodge. All these activities help develop coordination. A rolling ball comes toward a child and he kicks it. Another child runs to catch it. Both are developing an internal synchrony, for their movements, to be effective, must mesh in time and place with the changing position of the ball. A child who consistently kicks too soon or too late or a child who consistently misses catching a ball is going to need help. The same can be said of the child who throws awkwardly, stiffly, or erratically. The perceptive teacher may be able to watch a group playing kickball, and pick out some who will have learning problems.

Furthermore, the game has a structure, and children who play it are experiencing this structure with their own muscles. Some events can take place only in relation to other events. A player must kick the ball (within a designated area, lest it be a foul) before he may start running the bases. He may start from one base and run to another base only if he estimates that his chances of arriving safely outweigh his chances of being put out; and he may be put out in several ways. A player's relationship to the structure of the game is a dynamic relationship: At any given moment he must keep in mind where he is, where he wants to go, where certain of his teammates are and what they are doing, where the ball is in relation to himself and to other players, and where all the opposing players are and how their locations and future actions affect his immediate situation. Still more structure derives from the fact that the arena in which his activity takes place is a geometric pattern: a "ball diamond," which is more accurately labeled a square. In playing the game, he negotiates this geometric pattern. Thus, the structure is made up of elements which embody time, space, dimension, and form. In playing the game, the player experiences all of these elements, and has opportunities for developing and refining his own internal structure.

The game of kickball, then, will serve a dual purpose in this unit of instruction. It will be the experience upon which the experience chart is based, and it will provide some fundamental activities which should develop or enhance those perceptual-motor abilities which are essential to good reading. The main thrust toward perceptual training, however, will come through the teacher's use of specific perceptual-motor training activities which form an integral part of the unit. The teacher's observation of the children playing kickball probably will reveal some perceptual deficiencies which will require remediation. The unit offers guidance in detecting these deficiencies, and presents some remedial measures.

If the game itself provides perceptual-motor activities, why bother with additional perceptual-motor training? The answer lies in the fact that a game offers opportunities for development, but does not assure that a child will take advantage of those opportunities. A child with perceptual problems may perpetuate those problems in playing a game. Even more significant is the fact that a particular problem is not always solved in what seems the most obvious fashion. For example, if a child lacks rhythm in his movements, his basic need may be for adequate balance and posture; in this case, merely to encourage him to move smoothly will do little good. Children with perceptual problems typically have trouble mastering games. They experience frustration in attempting to cope with the demands for structure and skill which most games impose. Often they hang back because of repeated failures, and this practice becomes self-defeating. The unit therefore contains suggestions for certain specific perceptual-motor training activities designed for remediation of basic problems. These activities are so structured that they will provide far better perceptual training than does the game itself. A conscious effort has been made to present these extra training activities as a logical part of the unit itself, so that from the child's point of view they do not seem an artificial addition.

An experimental study by Rutherford (1965, pp. 294-296) tends to justify the addition of perceptual training *per se* to play experiences. In this study, forty-two boys and thirty-four girls in a church-sponsored kindergarten were divided through random assignment into experimental and control groups. Both groups played for 30 minutes each day under supervision of the investigator. For the controls, the period was spent in almost completely free play on typical playground equipment. The experimental group played on special equipment designed to aid development of perceptual-motor skills; this group spent approximately two-thirds of the period in free play and the rest in directed use of the equipment and activities. The activities for the experimental group were designed to develop the following basic skills: laterality, directionality, accurate body image concepts, visual-kinesthetic matching, and binocular and monocular control. The study investigated the effects of the training program on the readiness development of kindergarten children as measured by their performance on Metropolitan Readiness Tests. The study covered a period of 11 weeks.

Rutherford reports gains in reading readiness for both groups; however, the experimental group made significantly greater gains than did the control group. The following mean gains in reading readiness for each group as measured by Metropolitan Readiness Tests are reported:

Total experimental 4.3571
Total control 1.7857

The difference between the total groups was found to be significant at the 1-per cent level of confidence.

For purposes of presentation, the unit is organized into three broad areas:

1. Experience Activities (the kickball game).
2. Perceptual-Motor Training Activities.
3. Reading Activities.

While the unit will be presented and discussed in this order, it should be conducted in a different order. Soon after the Experience Activities have begun, the Perceptual-Motor Training Activities should be added and continued throughout and perhaps beyond the whole unit. Reading Activities (that is, preparation and use of experience chart or charts) may be added as early as the teacher thinks best, and continued as long as they prove useful. Once the unit is under way, therefore, activities from all three areas may be employed in a given day. This flexible organization for conduct of the unit should permit its use in a wide variety of teaching situations.

Under each of the above three areas, the recommended activities will be presented and discussed. In a separate but parallel column the teacher will find suggestions for detecting some basic problems and procedures for their remediation. Since the remediation is described in the second area, Perceptual-Motor Training Activities, the first area typically will contain references only to remediation which can be found in the second area; thus much repetition can be avoided.

UNIT: BEGINNING READING WITH EXPERIENCE CHARTS
Area 1: Experience Activities

EXPERIENCES	PROBLEMS AND REMEDIATION
Opener:	*Note:* Remedial activities will be indicated by roman numerals according to the following key: I. Activities for BALANCE AND POSTURE II. Activities for BODY IMAGE AND DIFFERENTIATION III. Activities for PERCEPTUAL-MOTOR MATCH IV. Activities for OCULAR CONTROL V. Activities for FORM PERCEPTION. In Area 1, typical problems indicating need for these remedial activities will be described so the teacher may be alerted for observation of certain behaviors. The key will be used to link problems to remedial activities; the remedial activities themselves are described in Area 2. As used here, the term "problem" refers to consistent behavior. Perhaps all behaviors described will occur at some time with nearly all children. Behaviors should be considered as problems to be dealt with only when they appear consistently.
1. Ask the class if anyone knows how to play kickball. Try to get a general, unstructured discussion going. The discussion should not bog down in details of rules, but should keep to the main elements: two teams, four bases (names of bases), runs, players, outs. If the game is known only to a few, tell them it is "like baseball"; this definition may widen the circle of those who have knowledge to contribute. Tell them they will be playing kickball, and that the class will write a story about things that happen in the game. Avoid detailed instructions; at this point they should be getting, through their discussion, a general picture of the game. Their later learning of the game should come about naturally as they involve themselves in it, rather than as a response to verbal structuring. This discussion should take place shortly before the game is played for the first time.	
2. *Dividing into Two Teams.* Division should be random, and the following procedure should be used: Form the class into a line facing the teacher. Have them count off in twos from left (teacher's right) to right. The first child says "one," the next child says "two," the next says "one," and so on. Strive for a smooth rhythm to the counting. With the children still facing in the same direction, go	2. In counting off, each child's contribution to the total rhythm is, for him, a combined individual problem of synchrony and rhythm. If the sweep of sound along the line is to be smooth, each one must call his number at the right moment. Calling the number at the right moment is a problem in synchrony. Knowing just when the right moment has arrived requires the child to sense the

Perceptual Training with the Language Arts

EXPERIENCES	PROBLEMS AND REMEDIATION
behind the line and, using a clear and normal tone, say something like the following: "I will say 'one, two, three, go.' When you hear 'go' all number ones will go one step to the front. Number twos will not move. Ready? One, two, three, go." Counting should set a rhythm so that the children will be able to anticipate when the "go" signal will come. Point out that the class is now divided into two teams. Now re-form them into one line by giving the same signal for number twos to step forward. Up to this point the children have moved only in response to an auditory signal, since the teacher was behind them. With the children again in one line, move to the front of the line, and have the teams separate at a visual signal. With this visual signal a visual rhythm (corresponding to the auditory rhythm of "one, two, three, go") should be developed. For example, teacher's right hand could be used for "go," and left hand could be waved three times as preparation. Or, three sheets of white paper and one of red could be placed in a line on the wall; teacher points to all four in rhythmical sequence, with pointing to red (last) being signal to move. Children should divide into different teams each day. When most children have mastered the counting off and are able to move into teams readily on signal, variations should be introduced. Such variations are extremely important in that they aid the development of generalizations. Patterns of activities develop instead of isolated or splinter skills. Counting off may be varied in many ways. Teams can have any of a variety of names instead of team	rhythm of sound before it reaches his position in the line. Only by sensing the rhythm can he anticipate the moment when he must sound his number. Children who speak too soon or too late, or who are otherwise confused by this activity, probably have not developed synchrony and rhythm and/or have failed to match auditory information to the motor base. REMEDIATION I and III. As teams move by command, be alert for hesitation, awkwardness, and directional confusion. Hesitation may indicate lack of synchrony; however, it may indicate vision or hearing problems. Note especially the child who responds markedly better to either visual or auditory signals. If a child has trouble only with auditory signals, help from the speech and hearing therapist should be sought, or another appropriate attempt made to determine if he has problems with auditory acuity. Poor response only with visual signals may suggest poor vision, or it may be due to consistent failure to integrate visual information with the motor base. Some children may have good visual acuity and still not have developed the ability to match the visual to the motor. Such children perform well until visual information is added to the ongoing activity, at which point confusion enters. For example, a child may be able to tie his shoelaces until he looks at his hands; looking then throws him off, and his performance loses smoothness. If acuity problems in both vision and hearing are ruled out, hesitation in moving on signal quite possibly is due to lack of synchrony (REMEDIATION I), poor body image (REMEDIA-

EXPERIENCES	PROBLEMS AND REMEDIATION
one or team two; the children would then sound out the team name instead of a number (red team; blue team; Dodgers; Giants; tigers; lions). The military method of counting off is a good variation: Every one turns his head to the left, and snaps his head to the front at the moment he calls his number or team name. Or the line can be changed to a column, and the children can count off from front to rear or rear to front. When they are in a column, the movement into teams can be varied by having them step left or right, or having one team step right while the other steps left (or, if in line, by having one step forward and the other back at the same time). Instead of stepping, the teacher may call for hopping (both feet, left, right). These variations and many others should be used.	TION II), or (in case of visual signals) poor ocular control (REMEDIATION IV). The problem could lie in one, several, or all these areas; the routine perceptual training outlined in Area 2 should shed more light upon which areas need attention. General awkwardness in moving suggests that balance, posture, and body image and differentiation of body parts all have some developmental lack. REMEDIATION I, II. Consistent movements in the wrong direction may indicate lack of directionality due to lack of laterality. REMEDIATION I, II.
3. *Preparation of the Playing Field:* Let the children place the four bases in locations where they think they should go. The so-called "diamond" is actually a square; distances between bases are all equal and each corner is a right angle. Begin by having one child place the bases. Ask others if they think the bases are placed correctly. If anyone thinks they are not, ask him to shift those which are in the wrong place. When the children are satisfied with the arrangement, show them how to check the locations. To do this, one line is needed as a reference line. The line between home base and first base can be this reference line. The location of these two bases can therefore be arbitrary be-	3. Laying out the bases involves the child in a number of perceptual problems. He must have an internal awareness of a square, and be able to visualize a large square on the ground where no guidelines exist. He must also have some idea of equal distances between bases and the angles at the corners. If he actually puts the bases in their locations, he must be able to translate all these inner awarenesses into appropriate movements organized into a sequence of events. If a child cannot cope with any part of the operation, he may not be able to perceive the figure itself. REMEDIATION V. If a child shows confusion in directions, he may have

Perceptual Training with the Language Arts

EXPERIENCES	PROBLEMS AND REMEDIATION
cause they determine one line from which all other lines can be located. The first problem is to find the direction from first base to second base. The desired direction is one which will be at right angles with the line from home to first. Have one child stand at home base simply to mark the location. Another child should stand at first base; this child will be the controller. A third child stands at the approximate location of second base, and will move right or left as directed by the controller on first base. While standing on first base, the controller raises both arms straight up and out from his sides until they are horizontal. He then shifts his body around until his arms are parallel with the line from home to first base. He can check this orientation by sighting along his left arm, aligning it with the child who is standing at home. He should shift his feet and not twist his trunk in making these adjustments; the arms should be at right angles to the feet at all times. When the controller's arms are oriented properly, he should turn his head directly to his front. He is then looking generally in the direction of the child who is standing at the approximate location of second base. The controller signals with the appropriate arm to tell the child in front of him to move right or left until that child is located in the proper direction of second base. At this point, the proper direction to second base has been determined, but the actual location of second base requires that the distance from first to second be the same	a basic problem in balance and posture or differentiation. REMEDIATION I AND II. If verbal counting cannot be matched to stepping, the problem may involve balance, body image, and the perceptual-motor match. REMEDIATION I, II, III.

PROBLEMS AND REMEDIATION

EXPERIENCES

as the distance from home to first. The child standing at home can step off the distance to first base. He should walk with even steps, and should count his steps aloud. He steps the same number of steps in the direction to second base; at the end of his stepping will be the location of the second base. The procedure is repeated to locate third base; the controller now stands at second with one child at first and another at the approximate location of third. When all bases have been positioned, a check on accuracy may be made by stepping the diagonal distances from home to second and from third to first; these two distances should be equal. The pitcher should stand halfway between home and second base and also halfway between first and third. Whenever a pitcher takes his place, he should be required to align himself with respect to the diagonal lines; this aligning will provide valuable experience in spatial orientation.

The bases should be laid out in this manner each time the game is played. Rotate the tasks of positioning bases so that all have an opportunity to be the controller and to perform the tasks of stepping off distances. The distance between bases has not been specified; the teacher should adjust this to suit needs of the children.

For the first few times the game is played, or until the children have an adequate grasp of the game's structure, the bases should be in the same general area of the playground (or gym). After this initial period, different areas for playing should be selected each time, and the orientation should also be varied. Variation will aid generaliza-

Perceptual Training with the Language Arts 71

EXPERIENCES

tion. Thus, after learning the structure of the game in a particular setting and against a constant background, a child will experience the same structure against varying backgrounds as the field is changed from day to day. As he stands at home base on a given day, the school building (a major feature in the background) may be behind him; on another day the same building may be on his left, right, or front, as variations are introduced.

4. *Playing the Game:* The two teams should start play with a minimum of guidance from the teacher. They should learn the structure of the game from their own playing and their interaction with one another, with the teacher intervening only when they are in trouble. The teacher should give ample opportunity for some children to learn from other children.

While the game is in progress, frequent changes of player positions should be made. Such shifting of players should be according to a preset pattern, and each player should begin his movement to his new position on a common signal given to the whole team by the teacher. The following is a good pattern. At the signal from the teacher, the pitcher goes to the fielder's position farthest from first base. The fielder nearest first base goes to first base. The first baseman moves to second, second baseman to third, third baseman becomes catcher, and catcher becomes pitcher. All other fielders should shift slightly closer to first base to fill the gap left by the fielder who moved to first base. The children should be taught to

PROBLEMS AND REMEDIATION

4. In suggesting a somewhat inductive approach for the children's initial learning of the game's structure, the aim is to encourage exploratory activity. Some children will involve themselves in new activities more readily than others. The child who consistently holds back will need encouragement. Holding back may be a signal to the teacher that a child has perceptual problems. Typically, the perceptually handicapped child has trouble with games; he does not grasp the structure, he makes gross mistakes, and incurs the displeasure and even the scorn of his playmates. For such a child the game can become a threat, and he may react by holding back or engaging only in the most peripheral aspects where he is not challenged to use abilities he does not possess. Children who exhibit this pattern of behavior probably will profit from the entire spectrum of perceptual training activities outlined in Area 2. Their performance in these training activities may indicate specific areas of difficulty which will in turn indicate specific emphasis in remediation.

Changing the player positions also should help screen

EXPERIENCES	PROBLEMS AND REMEDIATION
move immediately when the teacher gives the signal, each child starting his move without waiting for other children. The teacher should give the signal with practically no warning. The signal could be: "Change positions! One, two, three: scramble!"	those children who have general perceptual problems, but this activity also will not be too helpful in pinpointing the specific developmental lacks. It should serve rather to alert the teacher to those children needing closer observation during perceptual training in Area 2.
This systematic changing of positions gives the child a varying task of moving with relation to the structure imposed by the game. He must not only cope with his present position, but must also be prepared to change that position in an orderly way. He must be aware, then, of the overall structure of the game, and not just the one element represented by his present position. Before the activity of changing positions is started, the children should have a good general grasp of the game's structure from their play experience. When this activity is first introduced, have them make the changes several times as practice.	The child whose general movements are stiff and awkward probably has not solved the basic problem of dynamic balance and posture, nor has he developed body image and the ability to differentiate his body parts. REMEDIATION I, II. The child who must give excessive attention to movement *per se* has these same problems, and will profit from the same remediation.
	Erratic and awkward throwing suggests poor body image and differentiation, deficits in perceptual-motor matching, and possible lack of ocular control. REMEDIATION II, III, IV.
While the game is being played, the teacher will want to be alert for the following performances which indicate possible developmental problems underlying perceptual difficulty:	Consistent eye-blink and/or ducking when catching the ball point to a lack in integrating primitive reflexes with other generalized movement patterns. The generalized patterns themselves may not have developed, or the integration may not have taken place. Activities under REMEDIATION I, II should reveal whether the problem lies in the area of lack of generalized movement patterns; activities under REMEDIATION III, IV should aid integration.
a. Stiffness and awkwardness in general movements. b. Excessive attention to the movements themselves. The child should focus his attention on where he is going rather than on how he is producing movement. c. Erratic throwing. d. Eye-blink and ducking when catching the ball. e. Kicking at the ball too soon or too late as the ball rolls toward the child; overshooting or undershooting	Kicking too soon or too late and overshooting fly balls suggest problems in synchrony, rhythm, perceptual-motor match, and ocular control. REMEDIATION I, II, III, IV.

EXPERIENCES

when trying to catch a fly ball.
f. Response only at the instant the ball makes contact with the player. Sometimes it is obvious that a ball moving toward a child is producing little or no visual anticipation of its arrival. The response takes place only at the instant of contact, and this response is more exaggerated and explosive because the child did not expect contact. The child seems surprised and the contact appears to startle him.

PROBLEMS AND REMEDIATION

Response only when the ball makes contact suggests problems in perceptual-motor match and ocular control. The key problem is that the incoming visual stimulation is not triggering a preparatory motor response. This problem points to poor perceptual-motor match. The problem is more complicated, of course, if poor visual acuity or poor ocular control results in distortion of the incoming stimulation itself. REMEDIATION III, IV.

The Experience Activities, or the kickball game, could take place on the playground or possibly in the gym. The Perceptual-Motor Training Activities are presented under two headings: one for those activities which require the gym, and another for classroom activities. The Reading Activities, of course, take place in the classroom, although, in a larger sense, all the activities in all the other areas are actually reading activities in that they are aimed at improving readiness.

A number of references to *The Slow Learner in the Classroom* by N. C. Kephart appear in Area 2. To avoid repetition, reference to this work has been abbreviated as "SL" followed by a parenthetical notation of page numbers. This unit may be enriched by using additional training activities described by Dr. Kephart in Part III of his book.

Area 2: Perceptual Training Activities

Perceptual training activities should begin soon after the children have started playing kickball. It is highly desirable that these training activities appear to the children as a means of increasing their skill at kickball and as a means of helping them learn reading. Some of the activities will be interesting to the children, but others may seem pointless to them and will require motivation in the form of tying training to kickball and reading.

One obvious way of connecting training to the kickball game is to remind the children that all athletic teams must train for playing. Start a discussion about the different ways teams train, and make a definite point that training means doing many things other than just playing the game. The children may have some background knowledge about spring training of professional baseball teams, training activities of local football teams, and the like. The main point is that many training activities are different from playing activities, and that the class will have some things to do as training which are not the same as the things they do while playing kickball. Most children also are eager to read, and the knowledge that the training will help them read should aid motivation.

The perceptual training activities are divided into two subareas: One part of the training is designed to be conducted in the gym (Area 2a); the other part is designed for the classroom (Area 2b). A daily gym period devoted to the activities described in Area 2a is considered to be crucial to the success of this unit. The gym period should last for about 50 minutes each school day. If the class has a daily physical education period, the perceptual training (Area 2a) might be conducted during that time. If this cannot be arranged, an additional gym period for perceptual training should be attempted. If neither of these alternatives is possible, perceptual training activities under 2a may be attempted, with modifications, in the regular classroom. However it is done, the Area 2a activities should be conducted; they should not be omitted.

The children should wear gym suits or clothing which will permit them to move freely and to function on the floor or gym mats where they undoubtedly will get dirty. Old clothes which still fit well would be ideal, because the training activities in the gym will involve much wear and tear on clothing. Girls should wear slacks or shorts for the gym period. An advance note about clothing from the teacher to the parents will be helpful, and may even avoid some parental misunderstanding.

All children in the class should benefit from perceptual training activities; however, those with developmental lacks or whose performance of the suggested activities is poor will profit from additional individual activities. The teacher will notice some children who are having difficulty either playing kickball or engaging in the perceptual training. Such children will need additional time with those specific training activities which are designed to overcome their particular perceptual deficits. Some major problems were anticipated in Area 1, and the roman numeral key system ties observed problems to suggested remediation in Area 2. Additional problems will come to light as the teacher observes performance of the training activities themselves. From both areas, therefore, a number of children will be identified as needing additional training beyond the organized group routines in Area 2.

Providing more of certain activities on an individual basis for some children while the majority of the class proceeds with the group program is a problem. Those activities conducted in the gym will make heavy demands upon the teacher for supervision and coordination; little opportunity will be available for individual training. If a teacher's aide or other responsible adult is available for the gym activities, the teacher may be freed for individual work with children who need it. Older or more advanced children may be used to supervise some of the simpler routines, once the teacher has started them. If the teacher must conduct gym activities unaided, it probably would be better to work on individual problems during classroom time. Individual work will not require the large gym area needed for the group program. The teacher should review the gym program carefully in advance, and organize the activities around his immediate situation.

The trampoline is indicated for use in the gym program. This device is excellent for developing dynamic balance, coordination, and muscular control. Its use in this unit will require special planning. No danger exists if an adult is present and if certain simple safety rules are followed. An adult should be present, however, and this adult should give his full attention to supervising the trampoline activities. Another difficulty is that in a 50-minute gym period only a few children, perhaps six or seven, can be accommodated by the trampoline; if more are "run through" they will not have enough time to get the full benefit. The trampoline should therefore be viewed as a separate project requiring a block of time and an adult to supervise. Admittedly, this complicates the teacher's problem of organization. The trampoline offers such unique and highly desirable training that it is well worth the extra effort.

The writer has first-hand knowledge of a gym program for perceptual training which was conducted with first-graders substantially as presented in this unit. The children were enthusiastic about the activities. Their interest was keen and sustained. On the other hand, as one sets down in words a systematic presentation of the program, the descriptive details most likely will come over to the reader as a rather dull and depressing business. Perhaps nothing reads with more dreary monotony than an account of body movements, positions, activities, and the like. But when the details of the program, tiresome as they seem to our adult eyes, are translated into action on a gym floor, the children have a thoroughly delightful experience. What is more, they get good perceptual experiences.

Perceptual Training with the Language Arts

Area 2a: *Perceptual Training Activities, Gym*

ACTIVITIES	KEY	NOTES AND VARIATIONS
1. *Daily Warm-ups*		1. All activities should be varied each day.
a. Jumping: Children jump several times each foot and both feet.	I	a. Vary by using rhythmic patterns such as LR, LLR, RRL, LRRR, RLLL, and so on. While jumping is mostly for balance and posture, addition of rhythmic patterns will promote perceptual-motor match.
b. Body parts: Teacher says: "Touch your ears. Touch your knees. Touch your shoulders, and so on." Proceed through all body parts (eyes, nose, mouth, ankles, feet, hips, elbows, head, wrists). Child should use both hands for touching.	II	b. Vary order each day; children should not memorize an order, but should solve the problem of locating and touching a part on command. Watch for hesitation in moving to any part. Elbows and wrists may cause initial confusion because touching these requires child to "cross over" and touch right part with left hand and vice versa.
c. Imitation of movement: Teacher says: "Watch me and do what I do." Teacher then makes a variety of body movements, and children copy. Teacher may use movements in b, above, as one group of movements for children to copy. Use arm movements shown in SL, page 132, and vary by adding movements of arms horizontal and forward. Avoid duplicating the sequence, but be sure to include all three types of movements: unilateral, bilateral, and crosslateral.	II	c. Children should make prompt and sure movements. A child may mirror teacher's movements or may make one-for-one correspondence. Vary order each day, and vary content.
d. Differentiation exercises: Have the children move specified parts, performing specified movements	II	d. The goal here is to provide experience in the great variety of movement which is possible with

ACTIVITIES	KEY	NOTES AND VARIATIONS
with each part. Examples: Arms horizontal and out from sides, make circles by rotating entire arm; make large and small circles; repeat with arms to front. Raise one foot and move toes up and down; rotate foot by making vertical circles with toe, then horizontal circles. Touch each finger to thumb; move each finger independently; rotate each finger; flex each finger; make fist and open hand. Move head back and forth, side to side, and rotate head. Rotate hand at wrist; move hand up and down and side-to-side with wrist as the pivot point.		the parts of the body. The variations are practically unlimited, and only a very few examples are given. The teacher should plan for this activity by considering a given body part and all the different movements of which that part is capable. If a child has problems in moving his body extremities smoothly and flexibly, be careful in making corrections. Corrections should take into consideration the proximo-distal and cephalo-caudal developmental sequence. Thus, if a child cannot produce flexible finger movements, teacher should first check to see if the hand as a whole moves properly from the wrist; if this movement is not satisfactory, check his ability to move his forearm; if forearm movements still give problems, check movement of arm as a whole from shoulder; then finally check ability to move the shoulder itself. This direction of checking is the reverse of the proximo-distal direction, and should enable the teacher to identify that point beyond which the child has not differentiated portions of his body. In making corrections, the teacher should start at this point and work outward. If the teacher attempts to correct finger movements without regard to the developmental sequence, the danger exists that the fingers will be "splintered off" from the sequence, and will develop in isolation from the other parts to which it has close relationships. If a child has not differ-

Perceptual Training with the Language Arts 79

ACTIVITIES	KEY	NOTES AND VARIATIONS
		entiated his hand as a whole from his arm, then he should be helped with movements of the whole hand before attention is given to the fingers; similarly, if the arm has not been differentiated from the shoulder, then attention should focus on the arm before working with the hand. This precautionary note is most appropriate in the case of first-graders. Some of the earliest tasks which the school requires of the child involve his using his fingers and hands in ways which demand a high degree of precision. All too often, he is required to concentrate on his fingers and the movements they make in drawing, copying, or writing, without regard to whether he has differentiated in an orderly way those parts which are developmentally prior to his fingers. In trying to cope with these demands, he may come to use his fingers in a stiff and awkward fashion, and he may not develop adequately a functional use of wrist, or arm, or shoulder.
e. Exercises on the floor:		e.
(1) Lie on back, arms crossed over chest. Raise head and shoulders only, and look at parts of body which teacher designates.	I, & II	(1) Vary by having children look at designated places in the room. Designate places which require looking right, left, up, down.
(2) Lie on back, raise leg. Make geometric patterns with toes outlining patterns; leg straight. Make circle, cross, square, triangle, rectangle, diamond.	II, III, V	(2) Do with both legs. Vary size of patterns. Vary angle to which leg is raised. Letters of alphabet may be added to geometric figures if children know the alphabet.

80   Perceptual Training with the Language Arts

ACTIVITIES	KEY	NOTES AND VARIATIONS
(3) Same as (2), except child points to toes as toes move in geometric patterns. In pointing, arm should be extended fully, and the entire arm moves as finger follows moving toes.	II, III, IV, V	(3) Same variations as in (2), but add this important variation: Child points first with right hand to right toe; left hand to left toe. Vary by crossing sides: left hand to right toe and vice versa.
(4) Lie on back, hands under hips with palms to floor. Raise both legs, keep legs together, and move both legs as one unit in making patterns. Eyes follow toes.	II, III, IV, V	(4) Vary by having each leg move separately to form two simultaneous patterns. Vary directions of patterns; change from parallel to opposite directions.
(5) Lie on side, shoulders elevated and supported by elbow, legs outstretched. Raise top leg and make same patterns as above. Eyes follow toes.	II, III, IV, V	(5) Vary size and directions of patterns.
(6) Lie on stomach, hands clasped behind at small of back. Raise chest as high as possible, hold for a few seconds.	I, II	(6) With chest elevated, look right, left.
(7) Sit with knees drawn up to chest, arms clasping legs slightly below knees. Lean back until feet are off floor and balance on bottom. Rock slightly back and forth and maintain balance.	I, II	(7) Rock to sides; rock with rotary motion.
(8) Sit with legs crossed, hands under knees and grasping feet. Roll all the way back until back is on floor. Come back to original position, all the while maintaining knees to chest and hands to feet.	I, II	(8) While on back, roll right, roll left; maintaining knees to chest and hands to feet.
(9) Sit with legs outstretched and apart; lean back slightly and support trunk on out-	I, II	(9) Raise one hand or one leg at a time as teacher designates.

Perceptual Training with the Language Arts 81

ACTIVITIES	KEY	NOTES AND VARIATIONS
stretched arms with hands slightly to rear and palms flat on floor. Raise body off floor, keeping trunk and legs in a straight line. Hold a few seconds.		
(10) Sit with legs outstretched and feet apart, hands resting in lap. Pretend top of head is a pencil, and move trunk, neck, and head as a unit, with top of head forming geometric patterns.	I, II, III, V	(10) Vary size of figures; vary directions.
(11) Angels-in-the-Snow: For instructions on conducting this training see SL (230-233).	II	(11) To supervise a group in this activity it may be necessary to form pairs; one child to perform while the second child passes visual signals from the teacher to the performer. This pairing is suggested in case all children cannot see the teacher while lying on their backs.
2. *Obstacle Course.* The obstacle course should be conducted daily. Various obstacles, described below, make up the course, and each child negotiates each obstacle, going from one to the next without waiting for the group to assemble. Thus, at a given moment some children will be on each part of the entire course. Several children should be designated teacher's assistants, and one assistant should be stationed at each obstacle to pass on information about the obstacle and to assist where needed. These assistants can go through the course when the other children have finished. While most of the class is on the obstacle course, the teacher		2. The obstacle course should be varied in the following ways: Use a different sequence for the obstacles each day. Each child should vary his own manner of performance each time he goes through the course. He may, for example, go through forward one time, backward the next, sidewise next, on hands and knees, and so on. Each child should go through the entire course several times each day, using a different manner for each trip. Children should be encouraged to discover different ways of attacking an obstacle, the assistant offering

ACTIVITIES	KEY	NOTES AND VARIATIONS
may be able to work with those children who need individual help.		suggestions only when they have exhausted their own resources. The obstacles described below may suggest others to the teacher; such variations by the teacher will enrich the experience.
Elements in the obstacle course:		
a. Walking boards: Three or four boards can be used in the obstacle course to prevent a pile-up of children waiting their turn. They could be laid parallel, and a child would negotiate only one board for each trip. The walking board is a standard 2″ x 4″ board and from 8 to 12 feet long. Each end is fitted into a bracket which raises the top edge 6 inches off the floor.	I	a. See SL (217-221) for use and variations of the walking board. Begin with 4-inch side up and turn 2-inch side up on some boards as the children begin to master the larger side. Remember the goal is not to teach a highly developed skill, but rather to provide a variety of experiences where the child must solve the balance problem. Additional variations are stepping over or under a ruler held above board; walking with objects of different weight in each hand; balancing light objects on backs of hands; balancing book on head; changing from forward to sidewise, sidewise to backward, and so on; catching and throwing ball while walking the board.
b. Balance boards: Three or four of these also will prevent pile-ups.	I	b. See SL (222-224) for construction, use, and variations.
c. Climber: The climber can be any one of a number of climbing devices such as a climbing ladder, a dome-type climber, a climbing house, or similar device available from manufacturers in varied designs. The object is to provide an obstacle which requires the child to use hands, arms,	II	c. Have the children experiment with different ways of getting over the climber. Insist upon variations.

Perceptual Training with the Language Arts

ACTIVITIES	KEY	NOTES AND VARIATIONS
legs, feet, and many muscle pairs in going over. d. Tunnel: This item can be as simple as a long box made of corrugated paper board. A steel drum with both ends removed (edges smoothed for safety) will serve as well. A cloth mesh fastened to round wire hoops which fold in an accordion fashion is available commercially. The child goes through in a prone position, and gains an awareness of the space his body occupies, and an awareness of his body in relation to a definite amount of enclosed space.	II	d. Vary by having child go through head-first, feet-first, on back, on stomach, on sides, on hands and knees. He should discover these variations for himself if possible.
e. Barriers: The course should contain a minimum of three barriers: (1) A low object which the child steps over; (2) a higher object which he ducks under; (3) an object which he must avoid by going around. These barriers should be negotiated while the child is in motion; he should therefore begin his movement prior to his arrival at the barrier. This activity helps him develop generalized movement patterns in that he should learn to cope with the barrier without undue attention to the movements themselves.	II	e. Vary the means of locomotion used as the child approaches the barrier; that is, walking, running, skipping, loping, hopping, and so on. Some children will stop at the barrier before negotiating it; some will hesitate and break the movement pattern. Such children have not developed generalized movement patterns. They lack the ability to focus their main attention on the goal of movement and give too much attention to the movements themselves. These children will need extra help in all the movement activities in Area 2a; the teacher should therefore help them with phases other than the barriers alone.
3. *The Trampoline.* If the trampoline is available, it is suggested that one child at a time be working on it under adult supervision. In this way, an individual	I II III	3. See SL (224-230) for use of trampoline and variations.

ACTIVITIES	KEY	NOTES AND VARIATIONS
child may have some time on the trampoline several times each week, depending upon the size of the class. As children finish their turn on the trampoline, they could join the rest of the class in the ongoing activities. As previously noted, this excellent device for developing coordination should be used in this unit if at all possible.		

Area 2b: Perceptual Training Activities, Classroom

ACTIVITIES	KEY	NOTES AND VARIATIONS
Each activity in Area 2b is a small-group activity. A number of these group activities could be taking place simultaneously. The teacher may want to assign a child to a particular group, and move him from group to group, upon the basis of teacher observations of the child's perceptual problems and his progress in training.		
1. *Movement and Form.* Mark out a kickball "diamond" on the floor, using tape to outline the field. The "diamond" is actually a square, and should be made with each side about 10 feet in length. Put a book on each corner to represent bases.		
a. Space relations: Designate one base as "home," and put a child at this base facing second. Have him point to first, second, and third bases, and have him tell which direction each is from himself (right, left, front, as the case may be).	II	a. Vary by designating different bases as "home," thus varying the child's orientation to the room. Reverse the procedure by asking him, for example, "Which side of you is closest to third base?"
b. Auditory space: Station five children in the following player positions: pitcher, catcher, three numbered basemen. Place a sixth child at home plate facing second. When he has seen all the players, blindfold him. At a visual signal from the teacher (pointing will do), one player claps his hands once. The blindfolded child is asked to identify the player by sound.	II III	b. Let the children take turns being blindfolded. Vary by leading the blindfolded child to first base, facing him toward second, telling him where he is and where he is facing; then have children make sounds for identification. Also vary sounds by having players stamp foot, whistle, groan, and the like. A child should engage in this activity at all bases.
c. Form through movement: Have the child walk through the "diamond," keeping his feet on the	I, III,	c. Vary by changing means of locomotion: heel-toe while walking lines, sidewise while keeping toes

ACTIVITIES	KEY	NOTES AND VARIATIONS
lines. He names each base as he comes to it. All members of the group can use the "diamond" at the same time; one following behind another. Variations are essential, and all should be used.	V	on line, sidewise while keeping heels on line, and walking backwards. Reverse order of walking bases (from home to third, second to first, and back to home); however, emphasize that base numbers do not change.
d. Form through movement and auditory clues: Station a child at each of the four bases, and assign a distinctive sound for each child to make at the proper time. Place a fifth child at "home," and let him look in turn at each child on a base while the latter makes his distinctive sound. Blindfold the fifth child, face him toward first base, and have him walk to first guided only by the sound being made by the child at first base. As soon as the blindfolded child arrives at first base, the child at first base stops his sound, and the child at second base begins his sound. This signal tells the blindfolded child to change directions and start to second. He continues until he reaches home base.	III V	d. Children take turns being blindfolded. Reverse order of walking to bases. Start at base other than "home," and have child tell name of each base as he reaches it. Stop the child at any point, and while he is still blindfolded, have him point to designated players. He should identify players from his internal awareness of where he is in relation to the total form; only one player continues to make his sound while identification is in progress.
2. *Experiences with Form and Direction*		2.
a. Have each child in the group draw a square on a piece of paper; this drawing is done while seated at desk or table. Point out that we can use the square as a picture of the kickball field, and have each child choose where he would like home base to be on his picture. He should put a mark	III V	a. Vary by changing location of teacher's mark. Set up situations where one or two children are on base when the hypothetical ball is kicked, ask to which base the fielder would throw the ball, and have the child draw line to that base. After variations such as these with child seated, repeat the

Perceptual Training with the Language Arts 87

ACTIVITIES	KEY	NOTES AND VARIATIONS
next to home base. Teacher then goes to each child, places a mark on his paper in any location which would represent right or left field, and says, "You kicked the ball and the fielder caught it here (teacher's mark). He will throw the ball to first base. Draw a line from the fielder to first base."		entire activity with child at chalkboard; then with child on floor drawing with crayon or felt-tip pen on newsprint. For children who have trouble drawing the square in any of these positions, see SL (202-205) for remedial techniques.
b. Point out that the children have been drawing a square to make a picture of the kickball field, but that we call the field a "diamond." Show them how the square looks like a diamond if they turn their papers so that one corner of the square is pointing toward the chest. Have everyone do this. Now have them draw a "square diamond," shifting the paper so that they must use all diagonal lines instead of the vertical and horizontal lines used in the previous drawing of the square. No child should attempt to use diagonal lines until he has mastered the use of the vertical and horizontal lines of the square. Repeat activity of 2a, using the diamond as the picture of the field.	III V	b. Present same variations as in 2a.
3. *Ocular Training.* In SL (146-150), specific procedures for assessing the child's ability to control his ocular movements are set forth. Training techniques are presented in SL (241-257). Because of the extreme importance of functional vision in the school program, the teacher is urged to include both assessment and	IV	

ACTIVITIES	KEY	NOTES AND VARIATIONS
training of ocular control in this unit of perceptual training. The techniques are described in detail in SL. The teacher should study the above references carefully. Assessment of all children in the class should be made; training activities should be used where indicated.		

Area 3: Reading Activities

Construction and use of experience reading charts should be started soon after the children have learned the kickball game and are playing it with some degree of confidence.

As the children discuss some of their experiences with the game, the teacher should suggest that they make up their own story about what they have been doing. The children tell the story in their own words, and the teacher writes their sentences on the chart. This work should be a group effort with several children contributing different elements. As new experiences emerge, additional charts are made. The teacher can control, therefore, the number of charts and the times when their use is most appropriate in relation to other classroom activities.

In the early stages of the unit, a typical experience chart might look like this:

Today we played kickball.
We take turns.
We ran to the bases.
Jim made a home run.
The Tigers won.
We had fun.

When a chart has been made, the teacher reads what is written. The teacher's hand should sweep along smoothly under the line being read, not stopping under each word. Voice and hand, of course, should be synchronized with the written words.

When the teacher has finished reading, children who volunteer may read. A child may wish to read only one sentence, or perhaps only one word. The teacher may lead the discussion to a particular event and ask if someone would like to read about it from the chart. Children who may not be able to read a sentence may pick out some of the words, or they may be able to point out which sentence describes a certain event.

At a later time, the teacher should make a second copy of the chart on stiff paper. The second copy can be cut into lines or phrases or single words, forming cards for vocabulary building.

In writing the story from the children's own words, the teacher probably will need to do some slight editing, but this should not be so extensive that the finished product becomes the teacher's story instead of the children's. One problem with the experience method is that the children will use words beyond grade level. To offset this problem to some extent, the teacher may suggest simpler substitutes. Another difficulty with the method is lack of repetition of vocabulary. By unobtrusive editing, the teacher may be able to increase repetition. It is best not to strive for orderly structuring of sentences into paragraphs, but to write the sentences in the spontaneous order in which they come from the children.

Whenever the children read from the chart, every effort should be made to get the hand into the activity along with eye and voice. The experience method can be most helpful in emphasizing the left-to-right progression of reading. Children who have difficulty with this progression should have extra attention on activities for balance and differentiation (I and II) during perceptual training. The same activities, along with activities for perceptual-motor match (III), will help those children who are unable to synchronize the eye, voice, and hand.

chapter 4

Perceptual Training in a Science Unit

This chapter sets forth a unit in science for use in a special education class for educable mentally retarded children (EMR) of intermediate grade school age. The unit is designed to provide academic training in the science area of "Force, Energy, and Power," and concurrently to provide perceptual training as an integral part of this academic training. It can be adapted to the regular classroom if desired.

CONCEPTUAL BACKGROUND

The goal is to provide learning experiences on these five learning levels: (1) motor, (2) motor-perceptual, (3) perceptual-motor, (4) perceptual, and (5) perceptual-conceptual. The concepts of force, energy, and power have elements which lend themselves naturally to helping a child structure himself and his world. A discussion of these elements and how they will be used with the five learning levels follows.

Force is experienced by a child through his muscular efforts as he moves, changes direction and/or speed, and interacts with persons and objects in his environment. Such muscular effort produces data which the child comes to use as part of his motor base.

In many ways, the child *experiences* force; he has many and varied inner awarenesses of force.

Every force has two elements: magnitude and direction. A 10-pound object at rest is exerting a force in the magnitude of 10 pounds and in a direction named "down." Any force can be conceived of as a straight line with an arrow on one end to show the direction; the length of the line will represent the magnitude of the force. Forces act together in predictable relationships governed by logical laws; therefore, several interacting forces can be pictured as geometrical patterns made up of straight lines which go in various directions and even form angles. Force, then, is not only something which a child experiences; it is also something which can be pictured. The unit takes advantage of this fact by beginning with force which is *experienced,* and from this starting point leading the child to force which is *conceptualized.* The unit moves progressively through five learning levels as it goes from experienced force to conceptualized force.

Since magnitude and direction are fundamental aspects of the space-time world in which the child must function, forces can be used to inform his data-processing mechanism about some aspects of that world. At the same time, he can be helped to build a firmer base from which to make relative judgments concerning his future encounters with his world.

Other phenomena are often associated with forces: Sometimes a visual experience occurs along with a force, sometimes an auditory experience, sometimes a tactual-kinesthetic one. The unit attempts to capitalize on these concurrent experiences so that more than one sense avenue is used to obtain data concerning the same event.

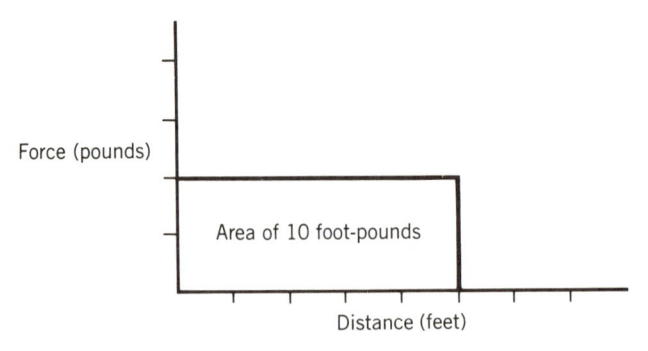

FIGURE 4-1.   **An Energy Graph**

Perceptual Training in a Science Unit 95

If force can be conceptualized as a straight line, *energy* can be conceptualized as an *area*. Energy is force acting through a distance; it is the product of force and the distance through which that force acts. If a child raises a 5-pound brick 2 feet off the floor he has exerted 10 foot-pounds of energy. A graph of this results in an area (see Figure 4-1).

In dealing with energy, then, a new element is added: distance. Distance also has magnitude and can be experienced. In exerting energy, in having energy exerted upon him, or in perceiving the expenditure of energy, a child is exposed to the magnitude and direction of force, and to the magnitude of distance. Each of these elements varies, but all are interrelated. They do not vary haphazardly; they vary in patterns. Reliable relationships can be experienced, perceived, and conceptualized. Patterns can be manipulated to set up many different situations for experience, perception, and conception; the unit offers some of these variations for the different learning levels.

The element of time is added explicitly when dealing with *power*. Power is energy expended in a given unit of time. Thus, dealing with power involves dealing with magnitudes, directions, and times. Situations may be structured where these elements are experienced as realities of the space-time world, where they are experienced in pattern and in relationship, and where each element can be varied at will and the variation experienced in the total situation.

The unit provides for unfolding these concepts of force, energy, and power hierarchically through the five levels of learning. At the *motor* level, the main interest is in providing opportunities for motor exploration which will increase the child's internal awareness of his body, and which will help build his motor base into a well-organized whole. At the *motor-perceptual* level, interest focuses upon opportunities to match the incoming perceptual data to the motor base. At the *perceptual-motor* level, the goal is to help the child project his internal structure outward upon the external data of perception so that he can structure that part of the world which is not immediately available to him. At the *perceptual* level, the motor can begin to drop out, and he can perceive without overt exploration. At the *perceptual-conceptual* level, he begins to deal with relations between perceptions without manipulating the individual percepts. In the unit outline, the content and the learning experiences are numbered from one through five to indicate the learning level. The divisions between levels are not sharply defined, and many activities will involve some overlapping.

CONDUCTING THE UNIT

The teacher should not expect that every child in an intermediate class for educable mentally retarded children will reach the higher levels developed in the unit; indeed, in many classes it is possible that none of the children will progress this far. However, children who cannot go all the way need not be dropped by the wayside. Even at the highest levels of learning as developed in the unit, tasks can be assigned so that all may share in the experience and gain perceptual training. The perceptual training in this sense can be had even if the corresponding higher level is not attained from this unit of study. What is unique about the unit design is this: The child interacts with a structured set of experiences, bringing into play a variety of sensory-motor mechanisms in the process. Interacting with this set of structured experiences provides opportunity for development of coordination. At the same time, the experiences are designed to teach the child something about the functions of force, energy, and power. He may not attain the latter goal, but attaining the former can aid his future learning of subject matter other than that in his unit.

The unit is presented in recommended chronological order. Three basic ideas are developed at the following learning levels:

Basic Idea I: Force tends to change the speed or direction of objects.
Learning levels:
1. Motor
2. Motor-perceptual
3. Perceptual-motor
4. Perceptual
5. Perceptual-conceptual

Basic Idea II: Energy is force acting through distance.
Learning levels:
3. Perceptual-motor
4. Perceptual
5. Perceptual-conceptual

Basic Idea III: Power is the rate at which energy is produced or consumed.
Learning levels:
4. Perceptual
5. Perceptual-conceptual

A simple numbering system for unit activities indicates the learning level which is most prominent for a given activity. The three "Basic Ideas" are designated by roman numerals. Each Basic Idea is subdivided into content areas and designated as "Content A," "Content B," and so on. Each content area is made up of unit activities, and each activity has a two-digit number with a decimal point separating the digits. The first digit indicates the learning level, as outlined above. The second digit merely designates the position of a given activity at a given level and content. For example, four activities under Basic Idea II, Content A, are at learning level 3 (perceptual-motor). These activities are numbered 3.1, 3.2, 3.3, and 3.4; in each instance the first digit indicates the learning level (3), and the second digit serves as a numerical listing of the activities at that level.

A SCIENCE UNIT: FORCE, ENERGY, AND POWER

Basic Idea I: Force tends to change the speed or direction of objects

LEARNING EXPERIENCES	EXPLANATORY NOTES

CONTENT A: *We use force to stop and start, to change from running to walking, and so on.*

Opener:

Tell the children, "We are going to begin a science project. We will do many things scientists do. (Classroom will be a laboratory at times, we will make measurements, do experiments, and the like.) Scientists study many things. Many times they study force and energy and power; we are going to study these things, too. We will start with *force*."

Development:

1.1 Have one child *push* a chair a short distance, then *pull* the chair back. By questions and discussion, establish that pushing and pulling are examples of force. Force was needed to start the chair moving. Let each child push and pull a chair, and ask if he can "feel" the force. Try to get several descriptions of what it feels like to push or pull; where the feeling is located and what it is like.

Materials: Basic need is space for walking, running; gym would be ideal, or outdoors if weather permits; if in classroom, clear large area. Several chairs (not folding).

Perceptual Training: Pushing and pulling an object gives training in differentiation (the muscular activity emphasizes that the arms are separate and distinct from other body parts, and that their movements are special to the arms), synchrony (starting, stopping, and reversing movements teach about "now"), and integration (to do the task, different parts must be coordinated in their movements to accomplish the goal):

Perceptual Training in a Science Unit

LEARNING EXPERIENCES	EXPLANATORY NOTES
1.2 "Let's do an experiment. How many different body parts can we use to make a force that will move the chair?" (Hands, fingers, wrist, elbow, shoulders, head, back, leg, knee, ankle, heel, toe, and so on.) Another experiment: Demonstrate body positions from which force may be developed to move chair. (Lying on back, stomach, sides; sitting, and the like.)	*Perceptual Training:* The major emphasis in this activity is generalization. By using many different movements to accomplish the same task, the children are helped to develop generalized movement patterns instead of "splinter skills." Movement of many individual parts also aids differentiation.
1.3 "We used force to start the chair moving; we use force to start ourselves moving." Have child walk a few steps, stop, and start walking again. Discuss: What "pushed" the child and got him moving? Could he feel the force in his legs? Could he feel the extra force in starting and stopping? (Avoid a precise locating of muscles; we want to avoid "splintering.")	*Perceptual Training:* Synchrony (starting and stopping) and differentiation (awareness of specific movement).
1.4 Use one child to demonstrate these four "speeds": standing still (zero speed), slow walk, fast walk, and run. Have each child change from one speed to another on command. Vary by using verbal commands, visual signals with teacher's hands, or four different colored sheets of paper (each sheet representing a command to change to a different speed).	*Perceptual Training:* Development of generalized movement patterns by varying means of locomotion. Development of synchrony by changing speeds upon command. Development of rhythm through rhythmical movements. Development of sensory-motor coordination by use of auditory and visual commands to control movements.
2.1 "We used force to change our speed; we use force to change the speed of moving objects." Roll a bowling ball, a volleyball, and a beach ball to each child, keeping the speed of each ball the same at this stage. Have the child use his hands to change the speed of	*Materials:* Bowling ball, volleyball, and beach ball (or other objects of different weights which can be rolled). *Perceptual Training:* Generalization (different weight balls are used), eye-hand coordination (hand movement must

LEARNING EXPERIENCES	EXPLANATORY NOTES
each ball (slow it, stop it, or make it go faster). Discuss which ball needs the most force to change its speed and why each is a different weight). Let each child feel the difference in weights by lifting the balls from the floor (watch toes with the bowling ball).	be coordinated with the visual monitoring of the moving ball).
2.2 Roll each ball several times at different speeds. Discuss difference in forces at different speeds. Vary by having children use different body parts to change speed of balls.	*Perceptual Training:* Primarily generalization. Different weight balls are now rolled at different speeds. Added generalization from use of different body parts.
2.3 Instead of teacher rolling ball, let children pair off and roll the balls to each other, varying speeds and body parts. (Because of weight of bowling ball, children should stand while manipulating it, standing and stooping to reach it, for sake of safety). At this stage, try to get across the idea that a big starting push requires a big changing or stopping push; that what we do to start and what we do to stop or change are connected.	*Perceptual Training:* Synchrony (starting and stopping), generalization (different weight balls are still being used), directionality (child must determine proper direction and roll ball in that direction), eye-hand coordination (required in starting ball).
3.1 At 2.1, we held speed constant and discovered that balls with differing weights required differing forces to change their speeds. Now attempt the more difficult task of having the child produce consistently the same force (by striking the balls with the heel of his hand, and developing the same speed at moment of impact each time), and observing the different effects this	*Perceptual Training:* Muscular control, monitoring of tactual-kinesthetic feedback.

Perceptual Training in a Science Unit 101

LEARNING EXPERIENCES	EXPLANATORY NOTES
same force produces on balls of differing weight. First have the children practice making the same force each time. They may use the heel of one hand to strike the other, practicing a "feel" of the same force. They may also strike the hands of fellow students and get verbal feedback regarding how consistently they produce the same force with each striking motion.	
3.2 When the children have developed a reasonably constant striking force, have them pair off and let each one use his constant force to propel the balls to his partner. The partner notes the receiving force (that is, the force he must apply to stop the balls), and in turn uses his constant force to send them back. Each child tells what happens to the balls when he uses the same force to make them move (some go faster than others). Each child describes how much force he used to stop each ball (this should be about the same).	*Perceptual Training:* Visual monitoring of varying speeds, together with concurrent monitoring of tactual-kinesthetic feedback from the muscular effort to produce the speeds. Generalization.
CONTENT B: *We use force to change our directions and the directions of objects.*	
1.1 Explain that we used force to change our speed and we also used force to change the speed of balls. Tell the children that we also use force when we change our direction and when we change the direction of objects like balls. Have each child walk and make	*Perceptual Training:* Directionality through changing directions. Directional changes develop synchrony and aid differentiation of those body parts which are activated in changing directions. Rhythm is developed through rhythmical movements.

LEARNING EXPERIENCES	EXPLANATORY NOTES
changes of direction, (left, right, reverse, half-left, and half-right) as he wishes. Each discusses what force he feels as he changes direction.	
1.2 Each child now walks in a circle. After all have done this, let the group discuss which side pushed with the most force. Now change directions of circles, and again discuss which side pushed the most. (In going in a circle, a child is continually changing directions, because he is moving away from a straight line at any given instant; hence, with each step he takes he is changing his direction).	*Perceptual Training*: Differentiation (muscles used are emphasized). Form perception (form is experienced through kinesthetic feedback from muscular effort in walking in a circle.)
1.3 Vary the two preceding experiences by having the child change directions as he runs, walks fast, walks slowly; do these variations by changing speeds in walking, in line, and in circles. A most interesting variation (and one which will aid the development of synchrony) is this: With the child standing still, have him start moving and make a change of direction at the same moment he starts.	*Perceptual Training*: Different movements help develop generalized movement patterns. Speed changes are for synchrony; direction changes are for directionality.
2.1 Use the bowling ball, volleyball, and beach ball for experiences of using force to change directions of moving objects. One child can start a ball rolling, and another can push it in a new direction. Children should learn that more force is needed to change direction of a heavier object and that, for a given	*Materials*: Bowling ball, volleyball, beach ball. *Perceptual Training*: Eye-hand coordination, generalization, synchrony, directionality, visual-motor monitoring.

Perceptual Training in a Science Unit

LEARNING EXPERIENCES	EXPLANATORY NOTES
object, more force is needed for greater changes in direction.	
3.1 We now want the child to learn how to control his application of force so that he can propel a moving ball in a desired direction. Several targets can be set on the floor; one child rolls a ball to another, and the second child pushes the moving ball toward one of the targets which the teacher designates. A child uses only one pushing motion for each assigned target. Use all three balls.	*Perceptual Training:* Eye-hand coordination, directionality, generalization, muscular control, monitoring of visual information from a moving object, synchrony, and monitoring of kinesthetic feedback from muscles which propel ball.
3.2 Have four children stand so that they form a square; each child represents a corner. Each ball is rolled around the "square," the children keeping the ball in motion by pushing (one push) from one child to another. If they cannot form the square by keeping the ball in continuous motion, let each child stop the ball when it reaches him, and then send it on its new direction to the next child. Give each child in the square a piece of newsprint and a crayon, and have him draw the square with the paper on the floor. Then have him go to the board and draw the square. Repeat the procedure with other geometric figures: rectangle, triangle, diamond.	*Materials:* Newsprint, crayons. *Perceptual Training:* The major perceptual training in this activity is form perception and generalization. Form is first *experienced* (rolling ball around the outline of the form), and then it is *produced* from two different body positions. A variety of generalization is provided in the activity: Drawing the form with newsprint on the floor and then drawing the same form on the chalkboard requires two radically different sets of muscular activity for the same task, thus promoting generalized movement patterns. More generalization is provided by drawing in two distinct planes; horizontal (floor) and vertical (chalkboard). (Many children cannot move easily from one plane to another.) Still more generalization comes from dealing with the same form in different settings: The form is first encountered as children forming the corners, next as a drawing on paper, and finally as a drawing on the

LEARNING EXPERIENCES	EXPLANATORY NOTES
	chalkboard. In addition to the major training in form perception and generalization, the activity offers several other obvious aspects of perceptual training.
3.3 "We use force to make our bodies go where we want them to go." Use masking tape to lay out several large patterns and geometrical figures on the floor. Have the children follow the tape markings by walking on the tape. When a child has completed one figure by walking through the complete figure (or pattern), have him draw that figure on newsprint and then on the chalkboard. Have the child label the figures he draws (circle, square, and the like), and engage him in conversation so that he says the name of the figure.	*Materials:* Masking tape figures on floor: Square, triangle, rectangle, diamond. Masking tape patterns as follows:

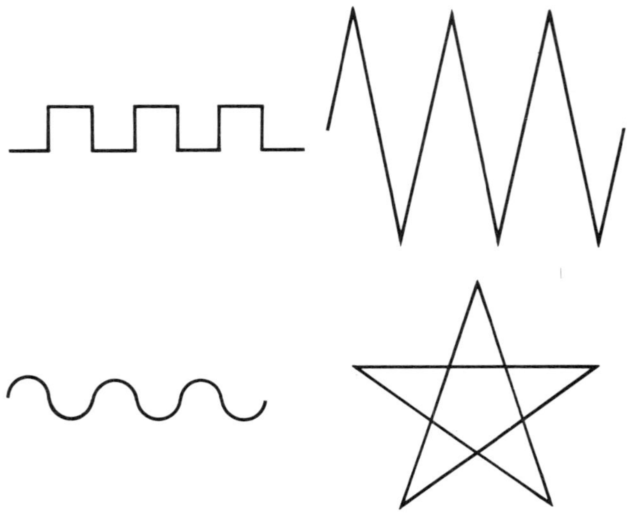

FIGURE 4-2.   Masking Tape Patterns

Perceptual Training in a Science Unit 105

LEARNING EXPERIENCES	EXPLANATORY NOTES
4.1 Draw a figure or pattern on the chalkboard, and have the children identify the corresponding figure (or pattern) on the floor. Children walk through the pattern after they have identified it.	*Perceptual Training:* This variation of 3.2 adds more of the same type training.
4.2 Draw a figure on the board, and have the children walk through the figure or pattern *without* using the masking tape lines as guides.	*Perceptual Training:* Previous activities have helped the child experience forms and produce those forms, both perception and production being aided by motor involvement. This activity offers training in perception of form through vision alone, with the opportunity to confirm visual perceptions with subsequent visual-motor experience of walking through the form which is outlined on the floor. Walking through the form also aids visual-motor coordination. Children who are unable to perform this activity should have additional experiences similar to those in activities 3.2 and 3.3.
4.3 Draw the figures on the chalkboard, and have the children draw the same figures on paper and then on the board. Then draw the figures on the board and erase. Tell the children to reproduce the figures on paper and then on the board. Next tell them to draw a figure as you call its name. Have the children reproduce these figures also on paper and then on the	*Perceptual Training:* Visual perception of form is confirmed by motor activity to produce the same form. This activity is to help tie the visual and motor avenues together. All the foregoing activities involving forms also aid generalization, since any one form is experienced in a variety of ways.
	Perceptual Training: This activity is mainly to provide more generalization. Having children draw after teacher erases copy is to add experience in recall (and gives the teacher a check on this performance). Note the variety of ways in which the children deal with form.

LEARNING EXPERIENCES

board. If children have trouble with any figures at this stage, have them walk through the figures and then attempt to reproduce them.

CONTENT C: *We use different forces to move objects which have different surfaces in contact. This is the concept of friction.*

2.1 Explain that round objects like balls move by rolling over the floor, but some objects are flat and must be moved by sliding. We will call the contact surface the "sliding part." Sliding parts can be made of many different materials; different materials need different forces to make objects slide. Demonstrate this by having the children put their palms down on a table top and slide their hands while pressing down; repeat with handkerchief between palm and table top. Discuss differences in forces needed to move the hand in the two instances. Emphasize that the different surfaces (skin and cloth) made them use different forces to slide their hands.

EXPLANATORY NOTES

Perceptual Training: Mainly differentiation and eye-hand coordination. Insist that they watch hands while performing. The increased muscular activity will emphasize the arm and hand as distinct parts of the body. Some children will tense the whole body on activities such as this. Try to encourage those who do this to relax as much of the body as possible except for the parts which are exerting force. Careful observation of children on this activity will help pinpoint those who tend to tense the whole body whenever they activate any set of muscles. This general tensing of the whole body is most undesirable, because the movement of parts does not stand out sufficiently from the overall tension; thus differentiation is hampered. Training in differentiation will be much more effective if the child is taught to tense only those muscles needed for the task, while keeping other muscles as relaxed as possible. In this way, tension in the muscles which are working will contrast with, or stand out in bold relief from, the muscles which are relaxed and not needed in the task. If this contrast can be experienced, the child is better able to become aware of the movements of the differ-

Perceptual Training in a Science Unit   107

LEARNING EXPERIENCES	EXPLANATORY NOTES
	ent body parts, and thus to differentiate those movements from each other.
2.2 Have one child sit on a piece of cloth, while another child grasps one end of the cloth and pulls with just enough force to move the first child. Change to different materials and note difference in force needed for each material. Take turns. Point out the two surfaces, the floor and the material we sit on, and that the material slides over the floor.	*Materials:* Several pieces of sturdy cloth, at least 18 inches wide and 3 or 4 feet long; each piece to have different texture (burlap, carpeting, drapery material, plastic, or the like).
	Perceptual Training: Generalization, differentiation, and control of movement. The activity involving the hand in 2.1 is generalized by involving the whole body in the same type experience. Generalization also takes place as the task is varied so that the children experience different forces with different materials in the same task.
2.3 Vary the preceding experience by using combinations of different materials as sliding surfaces. One cloth can be anchored to the floor by two children standing on it; the second piece of cloth is then laid on top of the anchored cloth and the child sits on the second piece. The child who pulls does so by pulling on the top cloth and making it slide with respect to the anchored cloth. Children should always pull the same child, lest the differences in weights introduce a confusing variation.	*General:* This variation is most important. The children should experiment with these different surfaces until they can agree which is the easiest, second easiest, and so on, to the very hardest combination.
	Perceptual Training: Mainly generalization.
2.4 Have children slide bricks with different surfaces over a table top by pulling on strings tied around bricks.	*Materials:* Six ordinary bricks, the kind used in buildings, without holes in bricks if possible. Glue six different ma-

LEARNING EXPERIENCES

Then vary by placing one brick on top of another, holding bottom brick, and sliding top brick by pulling on its string. Keep string horizontal and parallel to brick edges so that force needed for sliding will not be distorted. Determine relative gradients of forces needed to move bricks with different surfaces in contact. Have children feel all surfaces and identify by touch and by name of surface. Children should exert just enough force on string each time to barely start brick moving.

EXPLANATORY NOTES

terials (sandpaper, construction paper, plastic, cloth of different textures, or the like) to the two large surfaces of each brick. Each brick should have two different sliding surfaces for variation; for example, glue sandpaper to one surface of a brick and another piece of sandpaper to one other brick. Tie string between the two prepared surfaces and around the brick, thus:

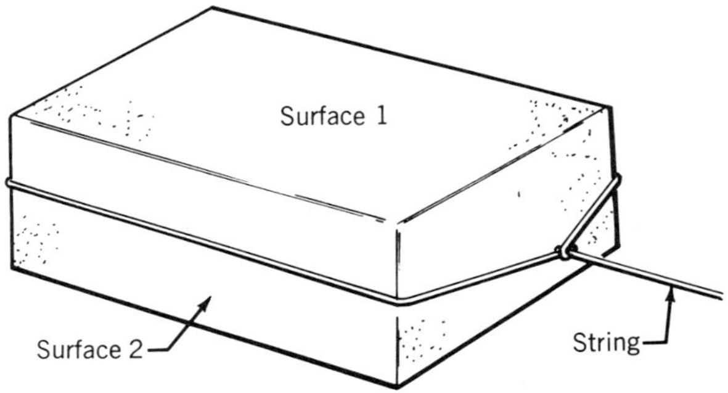

FIGURE 4-3. Brick with Two Prepared Surfaces

Perceptual Training: Experience in previous activities is generalized by changing to the new type activity with bricks. Experience within this new activity is further generalized by varying the surfaces to provide different forces from the same type of activity. In addition, some perceptual training takes place in differentiation of arm

Perceptual Training in a Science Unit

LEARNING EXPERIENCES	EXPLANATORY NOTES
	and hand as well as hand-eye coordination. In this and similar activities, children should watch the parts which are performing in the tasks.
3.1 Weigh each brick and write weight on brick. Use spring scale for weighing. Explain that the *weight* of a brick is the *amount of force* that brick exerts when it is put on top of a table or floor; that is, a brick weighing 4 pounds pushes down with a force of 4 pounds, and it pushes down with this much force on a table or any other object we put it on. We can tell how much force the brick is exerting by measuring the force we must exert to lift it straight up. Let each child attach the scale to a brick, raise the brick from its resting place, and read on the scale how much force he exerted to do so. Let each child also feel this force by placing a brick on his hand as the hand is resting on a table.	*Materials:* Spring scales. A convenient scale for this purpose is the kind sold by sporting goods stores for weighing fish. One popular model is known as a "Fisherman's De-Liar," and contains a flexible steel tape which rolls into the scale itself when not in use. This steel tape feature will be useful for later portions of the unit. The "Fisherman's De-Liar" comes in two sizes: one will weigh up to 16 pounds; the other up to 8 pounds. The smaller size should be adequate for most of the experiences outlined here, and is somewhat easier to read. *Perceptual Training:* Generalization and differentiation. Children are also helped to learn about the visual symbols which indicate weights; experiencing a connection between the symbol and the muscles needed to lift the brick. The unit offers many similar opportunities which are considered extremely important for children with learning disorders.
CONTENT D: *We can draw a picture of a force by using a line. The size of the force is shown by the length of the line, and the direction of the line is the direction of the force.*	
4.1 Explain that we can draw a picture of a force by drawing a straight line; the length of the line shows	*Perceptual Training:* The major training in this activity is for the child to generalize from an experience of a force

LEARNING EXPERIENCES	EXPLANATORY NOTES
how much force, and the direction of the line shows the direction of the force. Draw a vertical line 4 inches long on the chalkboard, and explain that we will let this be a picture of 1 pound. Draw a long vertical line close to the "1-pound" line, and have one child read the weight of any one brick. Then, have a child measure the weight of the brick on the long line by marking the length of the 1-pound line on the edge of a piece of paper, and marking this length on the long line as many times as there are pounds in the brick. If the brick weighs 4 pounds, he would have four lengths of 4 inches each marked off on the long line. Erase the excess of the long line, and put an arrow at the bottom to show "down." Underscore the fact that the long line with the arrow is a picture of the force of the brick pushing down on the table. The line is drawn with an arrow pointing down to show the direction of the force, and we made the line "4 pounds long," for example, by measuring the weight of the brick on the line. We cannot see the force but we can feel it when we pick up the brick. We can feel how much force and we can feel the direction of the force. (See Figure 4-4.)	to a visual symbol of the force. His experience of various forces has been in terms of the kinesthetic feedback from muscles as they encountered various forces. This con-

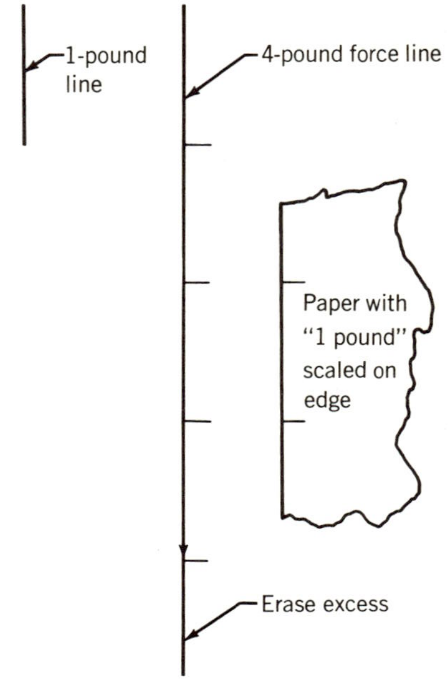

FIGURE 4-4. **Scaling Force**

Perceptual Training in a Science Unit

LEARNING EXPERIENCES	EXPLANATORY NOTES
	crete experience is now linked to the visual symbol. Many children seem to have difficulty connecting symbols with experience. It is important that each child be helped to make these most fundamental associations.
4.2 Have the children draw force lines representing the weights of the five other bricks, leaving a space of 3 or 4 feet between each line. Draw a "1-pound" line as a scale for each of the lines.	*Perceptual Training:* Additional experience of the same type as 4.1. Drawing and measuring gives training in eye-hand coordination.
	Materials: Spring scale and bricks.
4.3 Now demonstrate the fact that more than one force can act on an object at the same time. When the children slid one brick with respect to another by pulling on a string, two forces were involved: one vertical force (the weight of the brick), and a horizontal force (the force of friction, or the force of the pull on the string). To demonstrate this, set a table close to the chalkboard next to the force line of one of the bricks. Use only the brick whose force line is next to the table in the demonstration. Place the brick directly in front of its force line, and have a child attach the spring scale to the string, move the brick by pulling on the scale, and read the force needed to barely move the brick. The direction of the pull should be parallel to the chalkboard, so that the relationship of forces can be shown on the board more clearly. Now draw a horizontal line, beginning at the point of the arrow on the force line, and measure the amount of force	*Perceptual Training:* In pulling the brick along a horizontal surface, two separate forces are acting together: the weight of the brick is down, and the pull on the string is horizontal. The child can experience the size and direction of each of these two forces. He thus, in effect, can develop a kinesthetic figure in space through the information which comes through his muscles. The present activity helps him translate the "experienced figure" into a visual symbol of that figure. His muscles experience a relationship in space, and he translates this relationship into a visual figure in space. Along with this experience, he is receiving other perceptual training from muscles, eyes, and hands working together.

LEARNING EXPERIENCES	EXPLANATORY NOTES
needed to move the brick. At the end of this new horizontal line, place an arrow to show its direction. (See Figure 4-5.)	

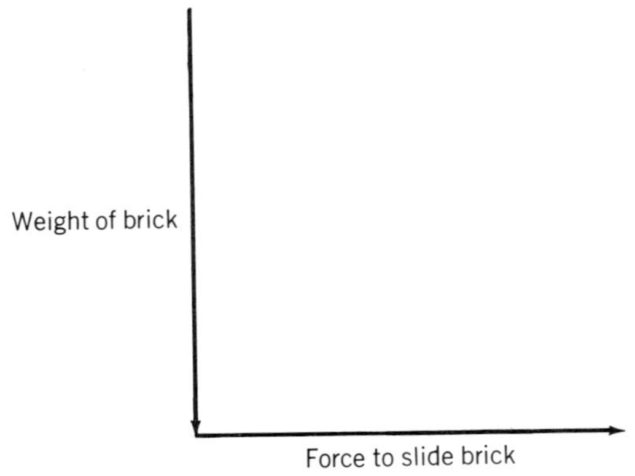

[Diagram: perpendicular arrows labeled "Weight of brick" (vertical) and "Force to slide brick" (horizontal)]

FIGURE 4-5. Two Forces on One Object

Perceptual Training: Mainly generalization. Some differentiation (from muscles in activities) and eye-motor coordination.

4.4 We have now demonstrated two simultaneous forces operating upon the same object. For any one brick, its vertical force will be the same, but the horizontal force needed to move it will vary as the sliding surfaces are changed. Have the children measure the sliding forces and draw force diagrams for the different forces needed to slide the bricks with varying surfaces in contact.

Perceptual Training in a Science Unit 113

LEARNING EXPERIENCES	EXPLANATORY NOTES
CONTENT E: *Forces acting together can be pictured as different shapes or patterns.*	
5.1 Each force diagram consists of a vertical force (weight of brick) and a horizontal force (sliding force). Each of these force diagrams are actually two sides of a right triangle. (See Figure 4-6.) Ask if anyone can see the two lines as part of a figure. When they see this figure, have them complete the triangles for all the force diagrams by drawing in the hypotenuse on each diagram. The figures should be left on the board or, if inconvenient, the triangles should be transferred to scale on large sheets of paper.	*Perceptual Training:* The children are now definitely into the perceptual-conceptual level; that is, percepts are used to help develop concepts. Force was first experienced through the muscles, then through visual symbols which represented relationships between forces. Through manipulations of a variety of mutually related forces, the child has the opportunity to form concepts of forces forming patterns.

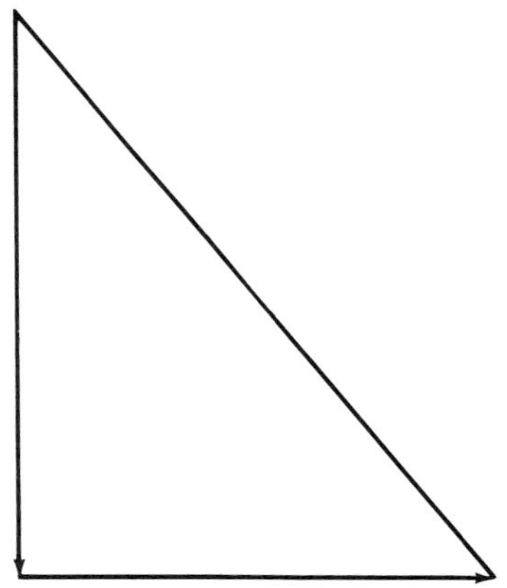

FIGURE 4-6. **A Force Triangle**

LEARNING EXPERIENCES

5.2 Possibly by now the children are beginning to conceptualize the two forces as forming a triangle. However, a much more important relationship can be demonstrated quite easily. Arrange a simple inclined plane so that the slope may be varied at will, and so that the vertical and horizontal components may be measured on the device itself (see Figure 4-7 for one way of doing this). Have the children set the board to the various slopes indicated by the various force triangles which they previously drew. For each slope, the surfaces corresponding to the force triangle should be set up on brick and board, and the angle at which the brick barely slides should be noted and compared with the corresponding angle of the force triangle. A very important variation is as follows: Set up two surfaces on the brick and board, and *without measuring* simply tilt the board to the position where the brick barely slides. Use the cord to fix the board in this position, and then measure the slope of the board and compare with the angle in the force triangle. (See Figure 4-10.)

EXPLANATORY NOTES

General: Each "force triangle" contains an angle which is the slope of an inclined surface, down which the brick will slide of its own free weight. For example, consider a brick

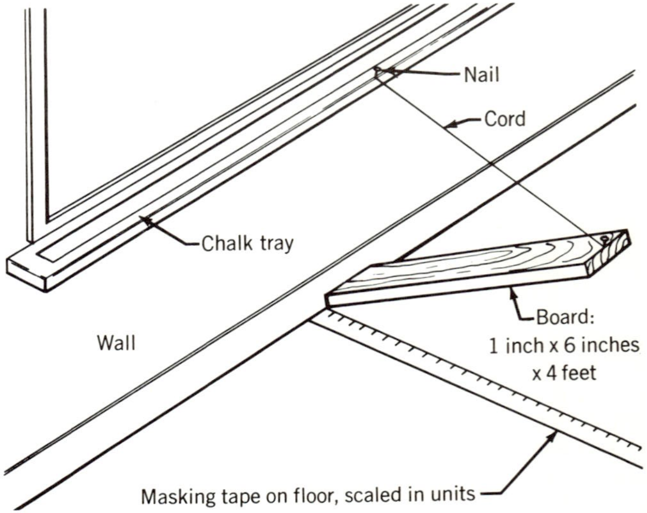

FIGURE 4-7. Making an Inclined Surface. In the example, the board is the inclined plane and its slope is changed by changing the length of the stout cord which suspends one end of the board in mid-air. A length of masking tape is stuck on the floor; the edge

LEARNING EXPERIENCES

EXPLANATORY NOTES

of the tape is placed next to the edge of the board when the board is lying flat on the floor. The tape can be marked off in pound units (1 pound equal to 4 inches is a convenient scale) and each pound is marked off into ¼-pound divisions (¼ pound = 1 inch if the suggested scale is used). The zero-point on the tape is the point where the tape touches the wall (or baseboard).

with a sandpaper surface resting upon a horizontal surface of paper. Assume that we pull the brick until it barely slides, and we find that it required 3 pounds to slide the brick. We weigh the brick and find that it weighs 5 pounds. We draw its force triangle:

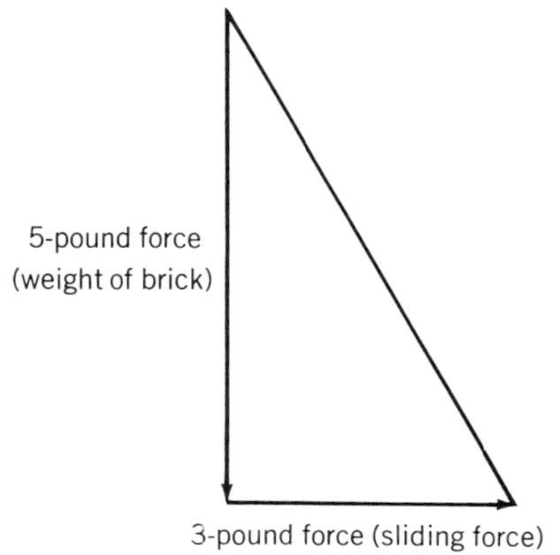

FIGURE 4-8. Force Diagram of 5-Pound Brick Which Requires 3 Pounds of Force to Slide It.

LEARNING EXPERIENCES

EXPLANATORY NOTES

We can then set up an inclined plane so that the slope of the plane is *three units vertically* for every *five units horizontally*, and we will find that the brick with sandpaper sliding against paper will barely slide down this slope. Note that each force triangle can be rotated 90 degrees, and the slope of the inclined surface is shown by the hypotenuse.

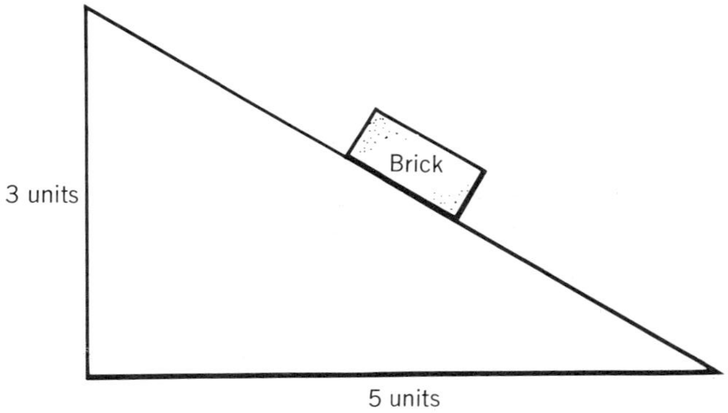

FIGURE 4-9. Inclined Plane from Force Diagram; Brick Will Slide of Its Own Weight

Assuming the brick weighs 5 pounds and required a sliding force of 3 pounds, first measure the 5-pound force on the scaled length of masking tape, and place a chalk mark on the floor at this 5-pound point. From this point,

Perceptual Training in a Science Unit   117

EXPLANATORY NOTES

LEARNING EXPERIENCES

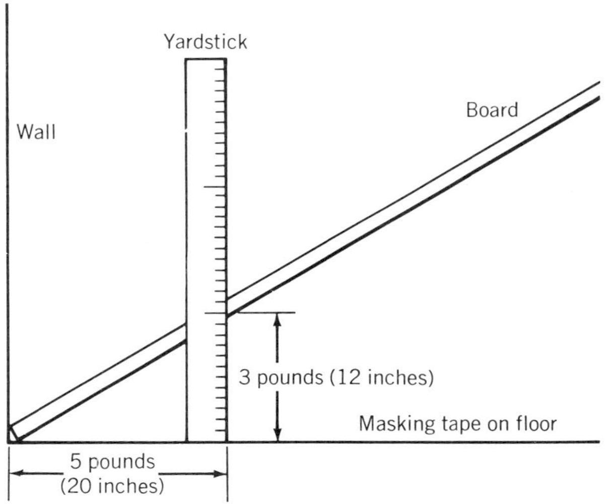

FIGURE 4-10. Measuring on the Inclined Surface. To illustrate the procedure, assume that we have a brick weighing 5 pounds which requires a sliding force of 3 pounds. We first measure the 5-pound force on the scaled length of masking tape, and place a chalk mark on the floor at this point. From this point, we measure 3 pounds straight up, and we adjust the cord so that the board is raised to the 3-pound (or 12-inch) point.

LEARNING EXPERIENCES	EXPLANATORY NOTES
	measure 3 pounds straight up, and adjust the cord so that the board is raised to this 3-pound (or 12") point. Since we assumed our force diagram was for a brick with sandpaper surface sliding on paper, we can thumbtack a piece of paper to the board and place the brick on the paper with the sandpaper surface in contact with the paper. The brick should barely slide. Bear in mind that our measurements of weights and distances are not as accurate as laboratory conditions would allow; therefore, it probably will be necessary to make a slight adjustment in the slope of the board to find the precise point at which the brick will barely slide. Our measurements are of sufficient accuracy, however, that the slope of the board will approximate quite closely the angle of the force triangle.

Materials: Carpenter's square, string, spring scales.

General: When an object such as a brick rests on a sloping surface, the weight of the object divides into two components: One component is parallel to the sloping surface and the other component is perpendicular to the same surface. The size of the two component forces depends upon the weight of the object and the slope of the surface. These two component forces can also be pictured as a force triangle, and the triangle will be a right triangle and will contain one angle equal to the slope of the surface. This relationship is illustrated by Figure 4-11. If the weight of the brick is drawn to scale, then the two components will also be to scale. |
| 5.3 Have the children set the board to correspond to one of the force triangles they have already dealt with, put the brick on the board (with proper surfaces on contact) so that the brick barely slides. Explain now that the brick slides because the slope of the board makes part of the weight of the brick shift downward in the direction of the board. This force is just enough to overcome the friction of the two surfaces, and so the brick will slide. But all the force of the brick's weight does not make it slide; some of the brick's weight is still pushing on the board. Tell them we will draw a picture of the brick's weight and the two forces it divides into on our sloping board. Draw a sloping line on the chalkboard, | |

Perceptual Training in a Science Unit   119

EXPLANATORY NOTES

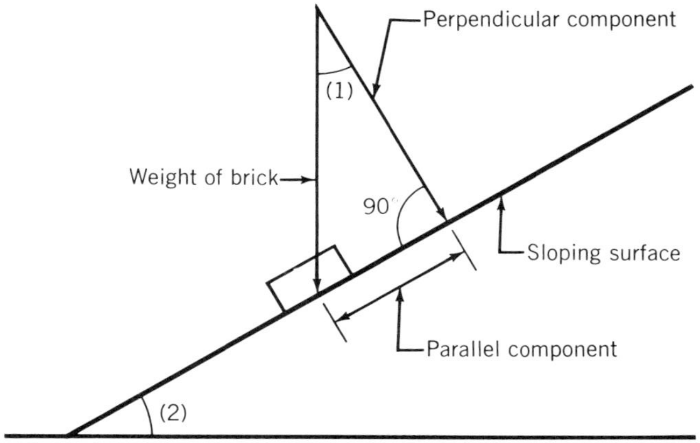

FIGURE 4-11. An Object on a Sloping Surface Divides Its Weight into Two Components — One Parallel to the Slope and One Perpendicular to the Slope: Angle (1) = Angle (2)

LEARNING EXPERIENCES

with the slope of the line equal to the slope of the inclined board. Draw a vertical line to scale representing the weight of the brick, and let this vertical line end on the sloping line as illustrated in Figure 4-12. Erect a line perpendicular to the sloping line and from a point at the very top of the vertical line representing the brick's weight. This line is the perpendicular component, and its scale length is the actual amount of force which pushes perpendicular to the sloping surface. The horizontal component is the distance from the perpendicular to the vertical line. The children should measure both of these component force lines, and should label each one according to the force its length represents. Now go back to the sloping board, and set the brick on the board. Put two thumbtacks (or other obstacle) into the board so that the brick cannot slide down, but so that it can be slid upward. Attach a string and a spring scale to the brick and have one of the children pull upward and parallel to the sloping board until the brick just begins to move; read the force on the scale at this point. Have the child then attach the scale to the brick so that he can pull in a direction which is perpendicular to the sloping board. He should pull in the perpendicular direction until the brick begins to lift from the board (the point of pull should be as near the center of the brick as possible). Measure the perpendicular force at the point where the brick begins to move from the board. The perpendicular and the parallel forces measured on the

EXPLANATORY NOTES

Measure perpendicular component

90°

Measure parallel component

Weight of brick (to scale)

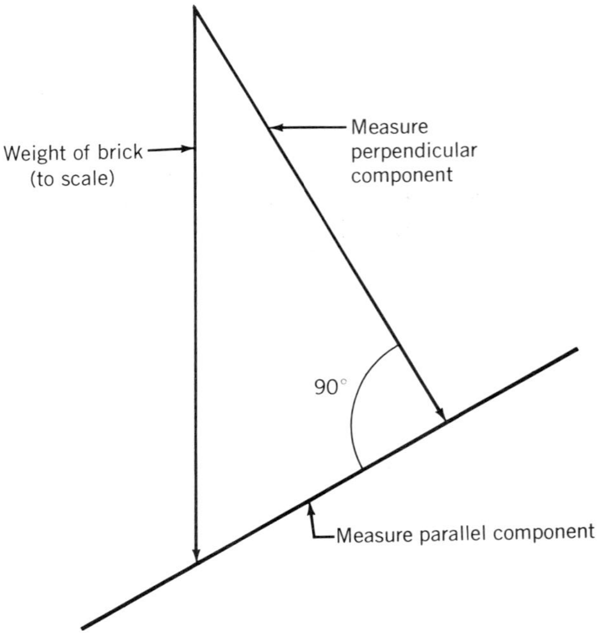

FIGURE 4-12. Constructing the Force Triangle for the Two Component Forces. Use large carpenter's square to draw the perpendicular line.

LEARNING EXPERIENCES

spring scales should be quite close to the amount of force measured on the chalkboard. Taking these measurements is illustrated by Figures 4-13a and b. Remember that the slope of the board should be consistent with the force triangle for a particular set of surfaces, and that the same set of surfaces should be used in this demonstration.

Perceptual Training in a Science Unit **121**

LEARNING EXPERIENCES	EXPLANATORY NOTES
	General: Use large carpenter's square to draw the perpendicular line. *Perceptual Training:* Note that in this activity the children must stoop over or sit down or perhaps even lie on one side in order to do the tasks outlined. These unusual positions mean that they do tasks in unaccustomed positions, and therefore they use different sets of muscles than usual. Most of their eye-hand activities, for example, are usually from a sitting position at their desks. Putting

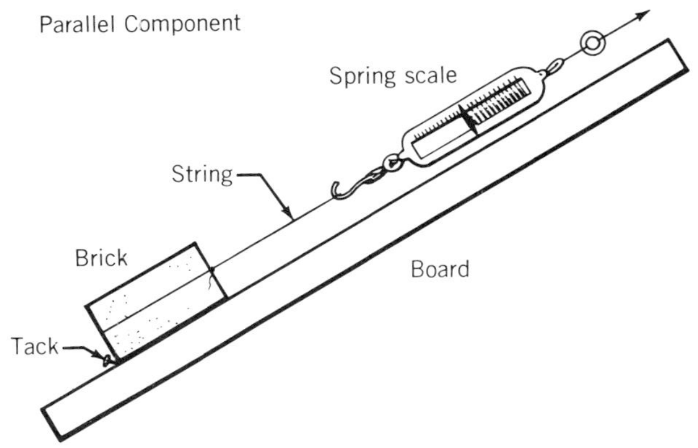

FIGURE 4-13a. **Determining the Components.**

122   *Perceptual Training in a Science Unit*

LEARNING EXPERIENCES | EXPLANATORY NOTES

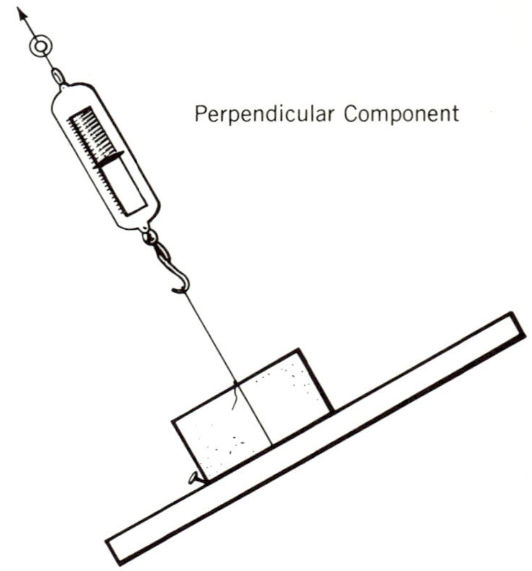

Perpendicular Component

FIGURE 4-13b. Determining the Components.

them in new positions for working puts new sets of muscles into play and helps promote generalized movement patterns. Other perceptual training has been explained in preceding sections.

General: Of course the teacher will not use terms such as "parallel component" in discussing these relationships with the children. Simpler terms such as "the force

Perceptual Training in a Science Unit

LEARNING EXPERIENCES	EXPLANATORY NOTES
	along the board" (parallel) and "the force *on the board*" (perpendicular) are recommended both here and other places where technical terms would be confusing.
	Materials: Two spring scales, string.
5.4 Explain to the children that when forces act together there is a balance; that is, all the forces in one direction are equal to all the forces in the opposite direction. For example, all the "up" forces must equal all the "down" forces, and all the "left" forces must equal all the "right" forces. To demonstrate this, suspend a brick of known weight from two spring scales, using string, and anchor the ends of the two scales to two table legs as shown in Figure 4-14. Point out the point of suspension, and tell the children that the brick is pulling down on this point with its whole weight of 5 pounds, for example. Now point to the two supporting strings, and tell them that each string is pulling up and to one side. Tell them that the suspension point is now not moving; all the forces on that point are in balance. The "up" forces in the two strings add up to the weight of the brick, and the "left" force in the left string is the same as the "right" force in the right string. Explain that we will draw a picture of the forces acting on the suspension point. Place a large piece of paper behind the strings, and trace in the three lines and the suspension point formed by their intersection. At this point, we are interested only in the angles and the suspension point. Remove the paper and tape it to the	*General:* Now it has been established that a given force can split off into components, and that these components have interrelationships and can be conceptualized as forming geometric patterns. Applications of this simple fact are

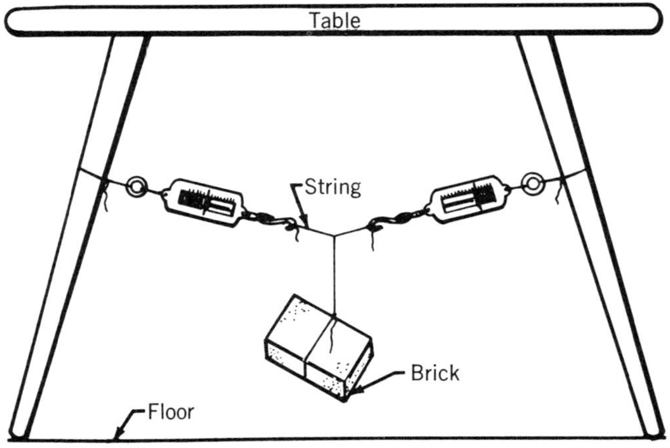

FIGURE 4-14. **Brick Suspended So That Forces of Suspension Can Be Measured.**

LEARNING EXPERIENCES	EXPLANATORY NOTES
chalkboard; the lines are in the same relationship as the strings from which they were drawn. Use a straightedge and go over the three lines to make them more uniform. Draw a horizontal line through the suspension point, and explain that the forces above this line are pulling up and the forces below it are pulling down. Have the children read the two spring scales, and measure off the number of pounds on the corresponding lines on the paper. Have them measure the weight of the brick on its line on the paper. A relationship to scale is shown by Figure 4-15. Call attention to the fact that the two supporting forces in the two strings add up to more than the weight of the brick, because only *part* of each force in each string is pulling *up*; another part of these two forces is pulling to the side. We can find out how much of the force in each of the two strings is pulling up, by drawing perpendiculars from the two supporting forces to the horizontal line as shown in Figure 4-16. Note that the two "up" forces of 2½ pounds each total the one and only "down" force. The amounts of forces in the supporting strings will vary as the angles are changed, but if the forces are measured to scale and marked out as this example has shown, then the "up" and "down" forces will be in balance. To complete our picture of all the forces acting on the suspension point, we need only measure and record the "left" force and the "right" force as shown in Figure 4-17. Have the children vary this procedure by using different angles of suspension.	limitless. The remainder of this section will consist of a few applications. *(Figure 4-15 shows a force diagram with a suspension point at center. Two upward diagonal lines labeled 5¼ pounds extend to upper left and upper right. A horizontal line passes through the suspension point. A downward arrow labeled 5 pounds (weight of brick) extends downward, and two lines labeled 5¼ pounds extend to lower left and lower right.)* **FIGURE 4-15. Force Diagram Drawn to Scale** *General:* Children need not add with numbers to find any of the forces; they can measure them all and apply the measured lengths to a scale such as the masking tape on the floor.

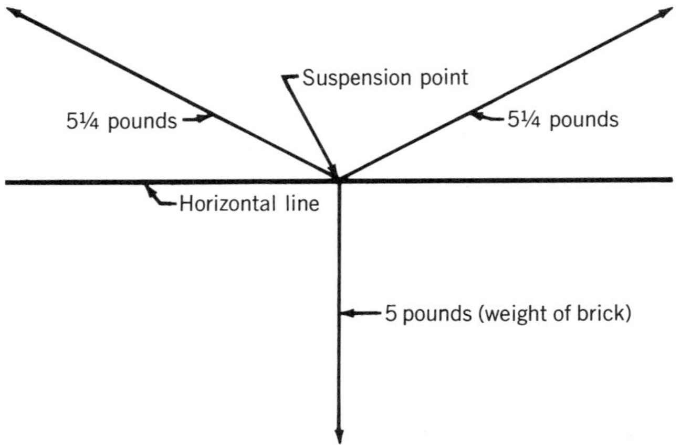

Perceptual Training in a Science Unit   125

EXPLANATORY NOTES

LEARNING EXPERIENCES

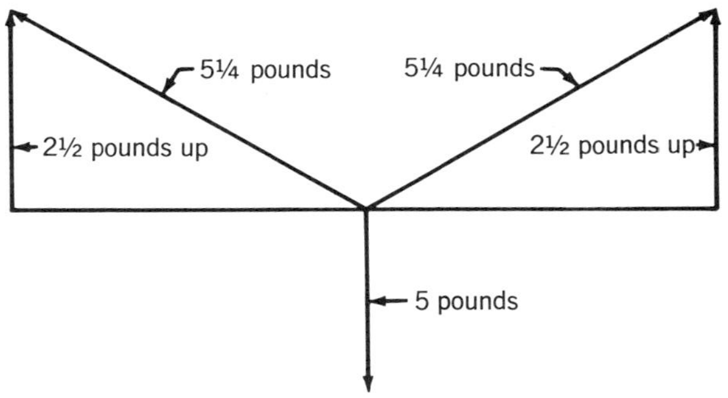

FIGURE 4-16. Determining the "Up" Forces; "Up" Forces = "Down" Forces (2½ + 2½ = 5)

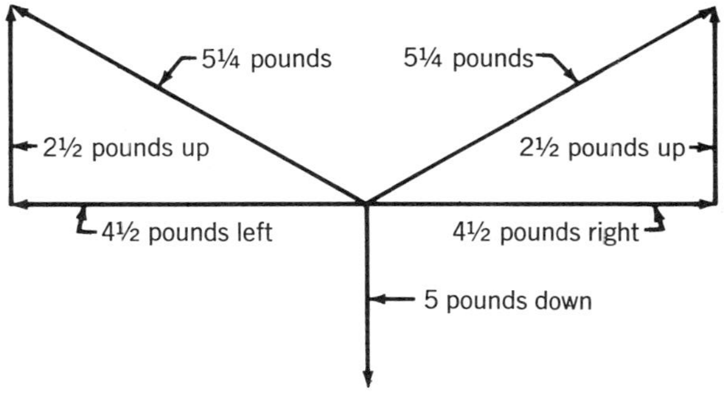

FIGURE 4-17. The Complete Force Picture with "Left" and "Right" Forces Added to the Previous Diagram

LEARNING EXPERIENCES

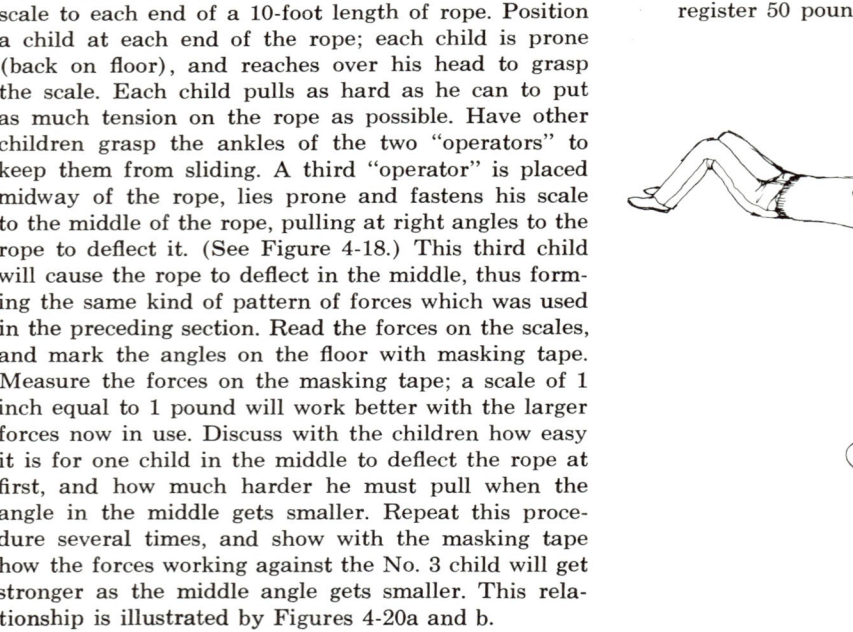

5.5 As a variation of the foregoing, fasten a heavy spring scale to each end of a 10-foot length of rope. Position a child at each end of the rope; each child is prone (back on floor), and reaches over his head to grasp the scale. Each child pulls as hard as he can to put as much tension on the rope as possible. Have other children grasp the ankles of the two "operators" to keep them from sliding. A third "operator" is placed midway of the rope, lies prone and fastens his scale to the middle of the rope, pulling at right angles to the rope to deflect it. (See Figure 4-18.) This third child will cause the rope to deflect in the middle, thus forming the same kind of pattern of forces which was used in the preceding section. Read the forces on the scales, and mark the angles on the floor with masking tape. Measure the forces on the masking tape; a scale of 1 inch equal to 1 pound will work better with the larger forces now in use. Discuss with the children how easy it is for one child in the middle to deflect the rope at first, and how much harder he must pull when the angle in the middle gets smaller. Repeat this procedure several times, and show with the masking tape how the forces working against the No. 3 child will get stronger as the middle angle gets smaller. This relationship is illustrated by Figures 4-20a and b.

EXPLANATORY NOTES

Materials: Three heavy spring scales, each of which will register 50 pounds; one rope, at least 10 feet long.

FIGURE 4-18. Forces Acting on a Rope

Perceptual Training in a Science Unit 127

LEARNING EXPERIENCES | EXPLANATORY NOTES

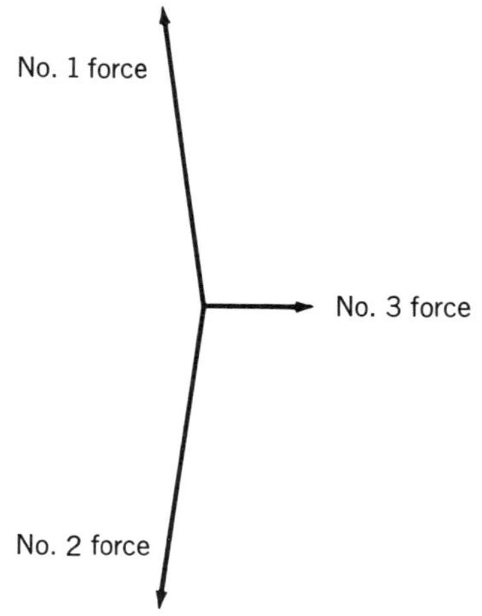

FIGURE 4-19. Diagram of Forces Acting on a Rope

LEARNING EXPERIENCES	EXPLANATORY NOTES
	Large middle angle — No. 1, No. 2, No. 3, Reference line, perpendicular to No. 3; used for measuring **FIGURE 4-20a.** Effect of Angle Size. Assuming that number 1 and 2 always pull with the same force, then the components of their pulling forces which are opposing the pull of number 3 become greater as the middle angle becomes smaller.

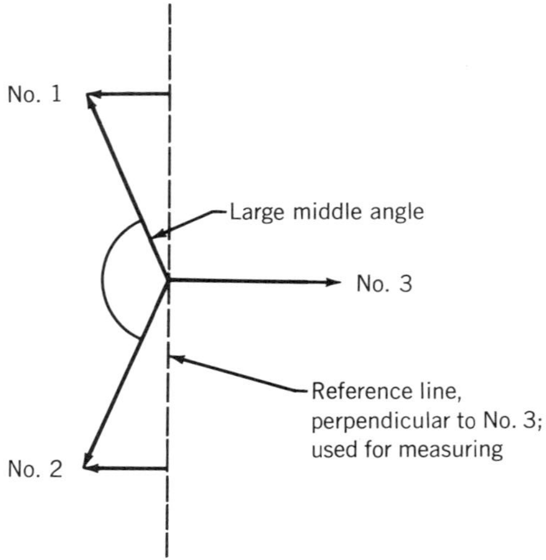

Perceptual Training in a Science Unit 129

LEARNING EXPERIENCES | EXPLANATORY NOTES

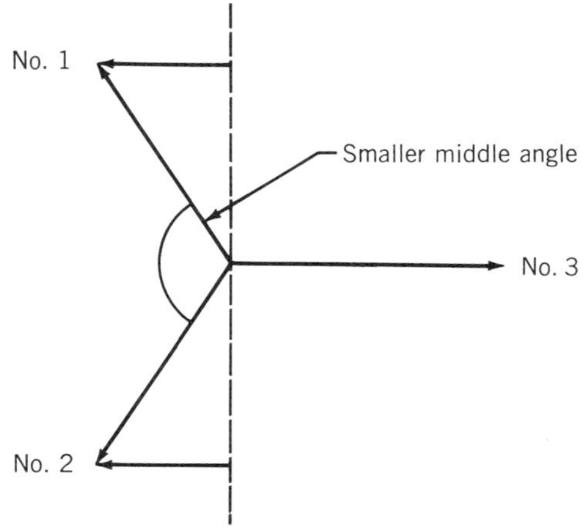

FIGURE 4-20b. Effect of Angle Size

(Figure shows three force arrows labeled No. 1, No. 2, and No. 3, with "Smaller middle angle" indicated.)

5.6 A most important variation can be had by reversing the procedures; that is, by observing only the force which No. 3 exerts, laying out the angles on the floor with masking tape, and measuring off the forces which No. 1 and 2 must exert to balance with No. 3. To do this, lay out the angles with masking tape, and scale off the distance of the No. 3 force. Use a string to find one-half of the No. 3 force, and move the line along the No. 1 force line until a point is reached where the

LEARNING EXPERIENCES	EXPLANATORY NOTES
one-half length of line will exactly equal the perpendicular distance from the reference line. Measure the length of the No. 1 force line; the scaled distance in pounds is the force No. 1 must exert. Repeat for No. 2. (See Figure 4-21.) Check measurements by using spring scales to read forces for Nos. 1 and 2.	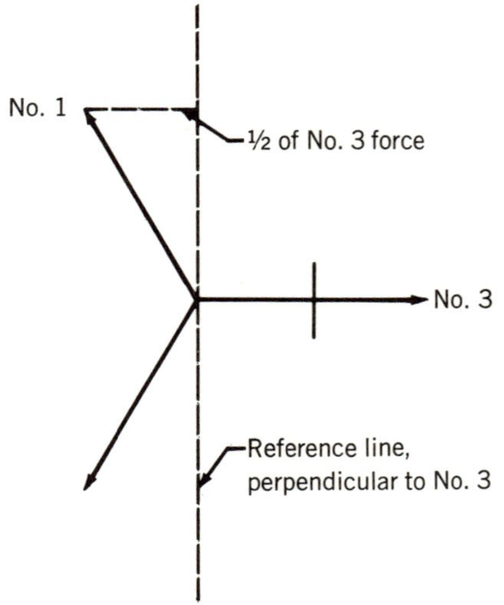 ![diagram showing No. 1, No. 3, ½ of No. 3 force, Reference line perpendicular to No. 3] **FIGURE 4-21.** Using Number 3 Force to Find the Other Two Forces. Finding number 1 force is illustrated. Repeat for number 2 force. *Materials:* Rope, three spring scales.

5.7 Still other variations can be provided by setting up hypothetical problems. Lay out only the three angles and a reference line, and assign an arbitrary value to the No. 3 force. Then have the children measure (as in 5.6) to find the Nos. 1 and 2 forces. Use the rope

LEARNING EXPERIENCES	EXPLANATORY NOTES
and spring scales to check the measured forces. This checking is done by having the children pull the rope until the rope conforms to the angles laid out in the problem. Nos. 1 and 2 pull until the assigned force is read on the No. 3 scales; then read the scales for Nos. 1 and 2. Have the children assume different positions as they pull the scales; sitting, squatting, and the like.	

Basic Idea II: Energy is force acting through distance

LEARNING EXPERIENCES	EXPLANATORY NOTES
CONTENT A: *Energy (or work) is the product of force and the distance through which the force acts.*	
Opener: Under Basic Idea II the children will be moving forces through distances, thus *using up energy* from their bodies. They can *experience* the energy output and they can *see* what this energy has accomplished. This relationsip between their internal experience and the observable external results should be discussed during each activity under Basic Idea II.	*Materials:* Various objects which the children can lift and slide short distances; scales and measuring tapes for weighing and measuring. Be sure to use the bricks and strings from the previous section. Chairs, tables, and other items in the classroom will serve.
Development: 3.1 Tell the children that we are now going to learn about *energy*. Energy is force moving through a distance. Have someone weigh a brick and lift the brick 2 feet straight up (a second child can hold a measuring tape so that the first knows where to stop). Assume the brick weighed 4 pounds. Now explain that the one who lifted the brick produced a 4-pound force which moved a distance of 2 feet; therefore he used up 8 *foot-pounds of energy*. Have the children lift or slide a number of different objects various distances, each time measuring the force and distance.	*General:* If multiplying numbers is beyond most children, do not spend undue time on arithmetic, since a different approach to this aspect of energy will come later on in the unit. *Perceptual Training:* Previous explanatory notes on perceptual training should make clear how such training is obtained from the activities outlined in the remaining portions of the unit. In order to avoid needless repetition,

Perceptual Training in a Science Unit

LEARNING EXPERIENCES	EXPLANATORY NOTES
	notes on perceptual training do not appear after this point.
3.2 One child sits on a piece of sturdy cloth and another child pulls him along the floor. Measure sliding force and distance pulled; compute energy in foot-pounds, teacher doing arithmetic for those who cannot do this. If weight of child on cloth is known, force triangles can be drawn as was done with bricks and string. Children take turns.	*Materials:* Large spring scales, rope, measuring tapes, and cloth which was used in *Learning Experiences* 2.2, preceding section. Tie rope to cloth and scale to end of rope. *General:* Once force necessary to start child has been measured, scale is no longer needed. This applies to all similar force measurements that follow; the starting force is the only essential force measurement.
3.3 Weigh each child on school scale, and record weight on chart. Post chart in semipermanent location where it will be available to children for reference. Tell children we will find out how much energy it takes to jump. Place a child next to chalkboard and mark his height. Have him jump as high as he can, and mark topmost height of his head. His weight multiplied by the distance jumped is the amount of energy (in foot-pounds) expended in one jump. Repeat with several children. Vary by computing energy for jumping on right foot, left foot.	*Materials:* School scale (nurse's scale), chart paper.
3.4 Now find how much energy it takes for a child to walk up a stair. Take children to a stairway, and measure the vertical distance from floor to landing. If this is not convenient due to construction of the stairway, measure the height of one stair riser, count the risers and multiply to find height. Have a child walk from floor to	*Materials:* Stairway (8 or 10 feet from floor to landing), measuring tape. *General:* This computation will result in some impressive sounding figures, for if Johnny weighs 70 pounds and walks a stair 10 feet high, he has put out 700 foot-pounds

LEARNING EXPERIENCES	EXPLANATORY NOTES
landing; multiply his weight by the vertical height (in feet) and the result is the energy he produces to walk up.	of energy. Some children may be encouraged to learn that they can produce something which sounds so grand.

CONTENT B: *We can draw pictures of energy.*

4.1 It is possible to arrange many different ways for the children to cause forces to operate through distances. A simple way to begin is to have them slide a brick by pulling horizontally on its string. They can measure the distance pulled and they can measure the force by using the spring scale. Explain how we can draw a picture of the energy, and let them measure off rectangles which will show how much energy they used. Note that now we are concerned only with *how much* force; we are no longer picturing the direction of the force.

General: In this section the children will, in effect, be drawing graphs indicating the energy expended or absorbed in various activities. These graphs will be in the form of rectangles (and combinations of rectangles). The unit will follow the engineering convention of measuring force in a vertical direction, and distance in a horizontal direction. The amount of energy is therefore shown by the *area* in a given rectangle, because energy is the product of force and distance and area is the product of height and length. At first use a scale of 4 inches to 1 foot; a square 4 inches on a side would thus represent 1 foot-pound of energy. For example, if a child lifts an object weighing 4 pounds and he raises it 3 feet in a vertical direction, he has expended 12 foot-pounds of energy. This task can be represented graphically by drawing a rectangle 16 inches (or 4 pounds) high and 12 inches (representing 3 feet) in length:

Perceptual Training in a Science Unit 135

LEARNING EXPERIENCES	EXPLANATORY NOTES

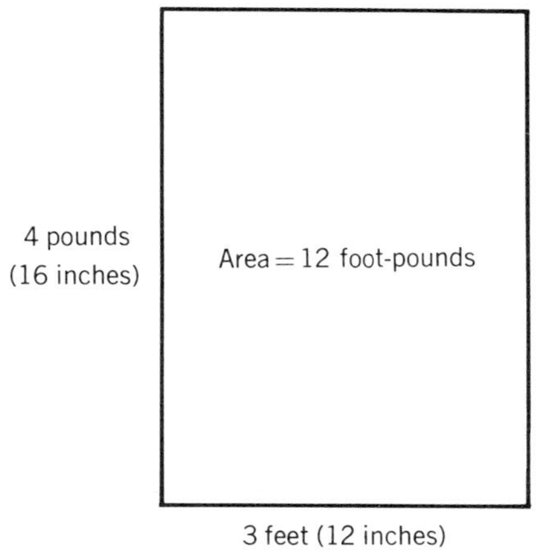

4 pounds
(16 inches)

Area = 12 foot-pounds

3 feet (12 inches)

**FIGURE 4-22. Example of Scaling Energy:
4 Pounds x 3 Feet = 12 Foot-pounds**

The area of the rectangle would show the energy: 4 pounds times 3 feet equals 12 foot-pounds. In the earlier stages of this procedure, it will be much simpler if forces are measured in whole pounds and distances in whole feet, thus avoiding cumbersome fractions.

4.2 Vary the procedure by having them pull one brick a few feet, stop and put another brick on top of the first one, pull both bricks a few feet, add still a third brick,

EXPLANATORY NOTES

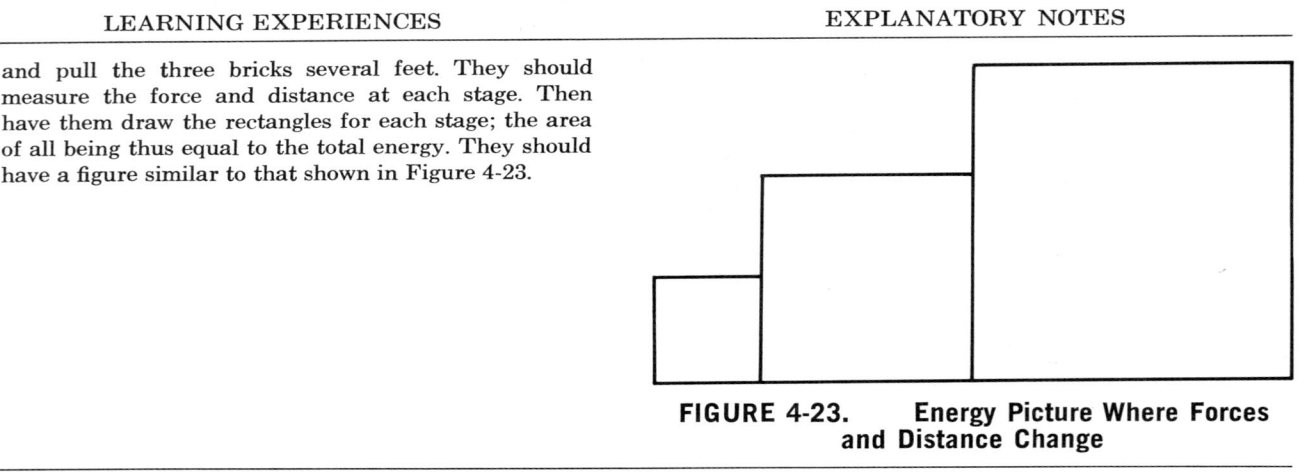

FIGURE 4-23. Energy Picture Where Forces and Distance Change

LEARNING EXPERIENCES

and pull the three bricks several feet. They should measure the force and distance at each stage. Then have them draw the rectangles for each stage; the area of all being thus equal to the total energy. They should have a figure similar to that shown in Figure 4-23.

4.3 Explain to the children that the same amount of energy can have different energy pictures, depending upon how the forces and distances combine. Twelve foot-pounds of energy can be made up of 6 pounds and 2 feet, 2 pounds and 6 feet, 3 pounds and 4 feet, 4 pounds and 3 feet, 1 pound and 12 feet, and so on. Have them pull two bricks for 4 feet, then four bricks for 2 feet, and draw the energy picture. The areas should be approximately the same, but the rectangles will look different. (See Figure 4-24.)

Perceptual Training in a Science Unit 137

EXPLANATORY NOTES

LEARNING EXPERIENCES

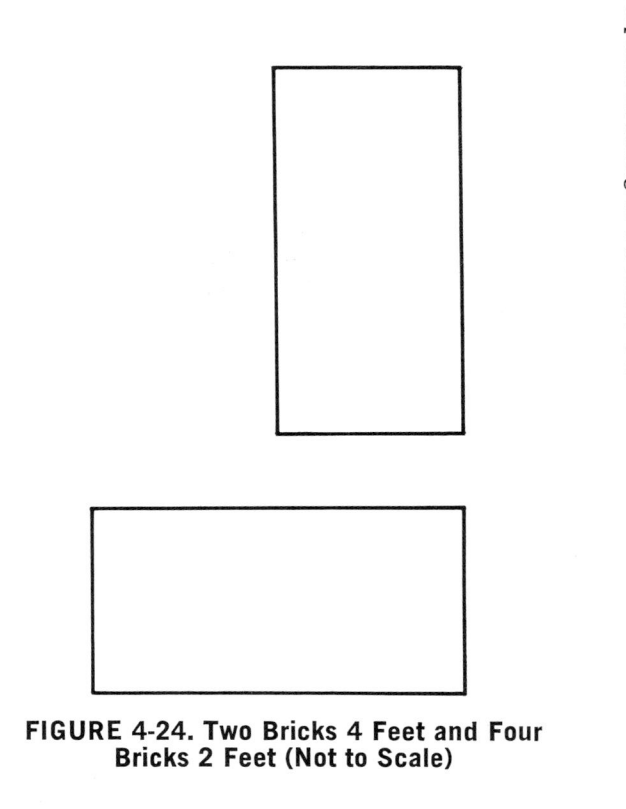

FIGURE 4-24. Two Bricks 4 Feet and Four Bricks 2 Feet (Not to Scale)

LEARNING EXPERIENCES	EXPLANATORY NOTES

CONTENT C: *We can change the form of energy, but we cannot create energy or destroy it.* (This is a crude statement of the law of conservation of energy.)

5.1 Explain to the children that when we put out energy, only the amount of the energy we put out is available to work for us; we cannot get more work done than we produce with our own energy. To demonstrate this idea, use an ordinary playground seesaw. Have one child (we know his weight from the chart) sit halfway between the fulcrum and one end of the seesaw. Have another child use a spring scale to measure the force which must be used on the other end to lift the child clear off the ground. (See Figure 4-25.) Once this force has been measured, the scale may be set aside. Have a child pull down on the free end until he raises the seated child 1 foot vertically. Measure also the vertical distance which the free end moved; this distance should be 2 feet if the seated child is at the midpoint of his end of the seesaw. The force needed to pull the free end should be one-half the weight of the seated child; it will actually be slightly more than one-half due to the small amount of force necessary to overcome the friction at the fulcrum. If the seated child weighs 70 pounds and is raised 1 foot, then 70 foot-pounds of energy was necessary to raise him. If he is seated at the midpoint, then the force on the free end would be 35 pounds which moved through a distance of 2 feet; this expenditure is also 70 foot-pounds. Have the children lay out large energy rectangles on the floor, using masking tape

Materials: Playground seesaw, measuring tapes, heavy spring scales.

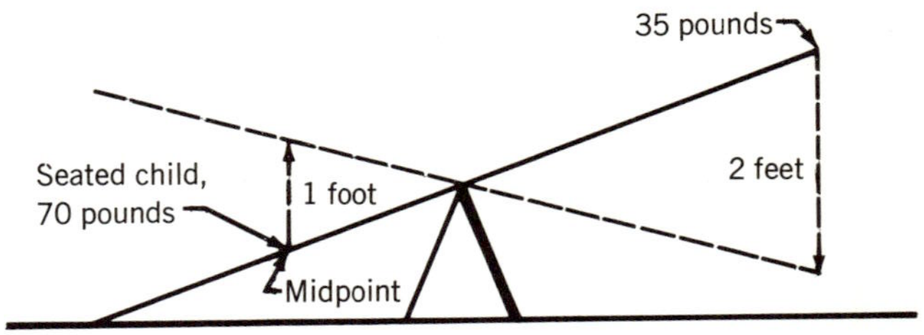

FIGURE 4-25. The Same Amount of Energy Is Produced on Each Side of a Seesaw, Even Though Forces and Distances Are Different.

Perceptual Training in a Science Unit

LEARNING EXPERIENCES	EXPLANATORY NOTES
to outline them. A scale of $1'' = 1$ lb. $= 1'$ will work best for this. Point out that the energy is about the same in both rectangles. (See Figure 4-26.)	

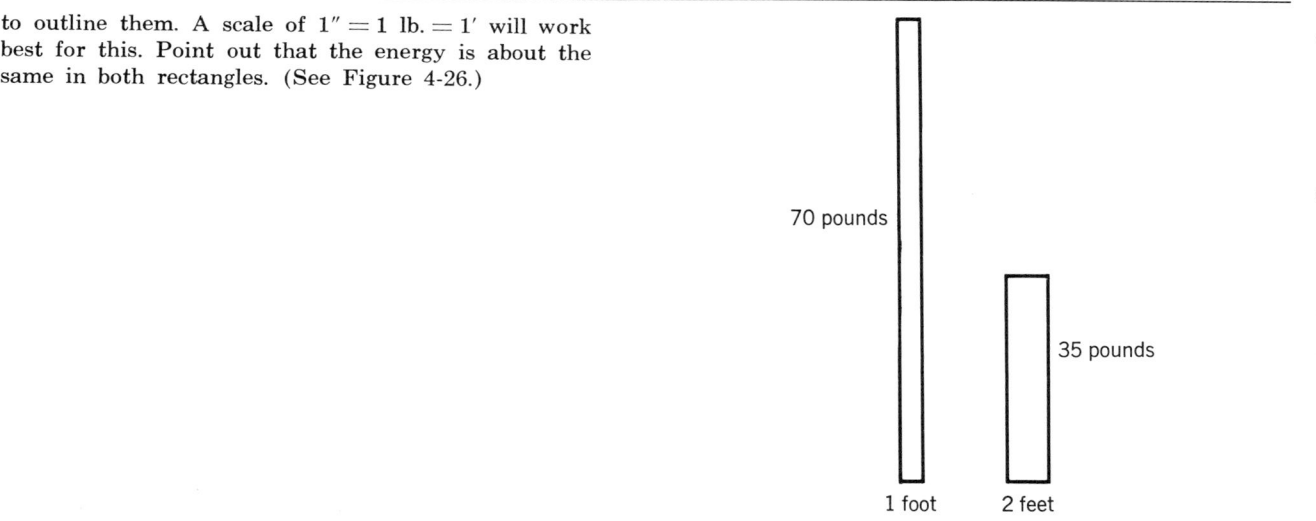

FIGURE 4-26. Energy Rectangles for Seesaw. Each rectangle contains 70 foot-pounds.

(70 pounds — 1 foot; 35 pounds — 2 feet)

Materials: Tagboard or heavy construction paper, scissors, rulers.
General: For small forces such as bricks, the scale $4'' = 1$ lb. $= 1'$ is recommended; for larger forces such as weights of children, a scale of $1'' = 1$ lb. $= 1'$ will be more convenient.

5.2 Point out to the children that on the seesaw we used only 35 pounds of force to raise a child weighing 70 pounds; thus we multiplied *force*. We saw, however, that the energy was the same on both sides of the seesaw; the smaller force moved through a larger distance, keeping the energy in balance. Since we have seen how

LEARNING EXPERIENCES

energy is made up of force and distance in many different combinations, we need a way to measure the space (or area) in our energy rectangles. Have the children make a number of "energy units" to scale from tagboard or heavy construction paper. To make an energy unit for the small forces, have the children cut out 4-inch squares, labeling a vertical edge "1 pound" and a horizontal edge "1 foot." (See Figure 4-27.) Energy rectangles can then be built by placing the units in the appropriate columns (for force) and rows (for distance). (See Figure 4-28.)

EXPLANATORY NOTES

General: For example, if a force of 6 pounds operates through a distance of 3 feet, we could make the energy rectangle by arranging the units as shown in Figure 4-28.

General: Determining the area (18 foot-pounds) can be done several obvious ways at the teacher's discretion. For the larger forces, make the energy "units" 10 inches long

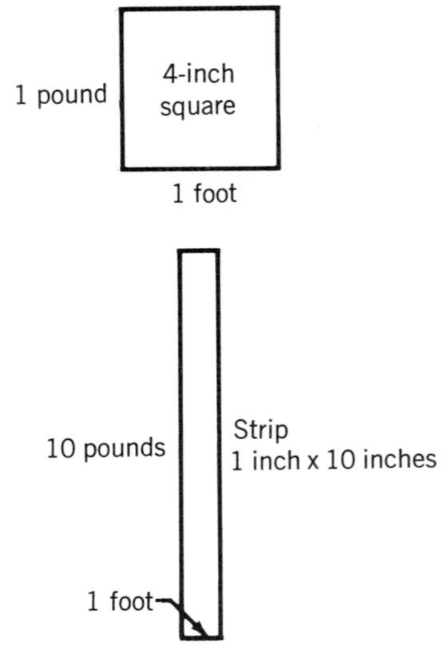

FIGURE 4-27. Energy Units

Perceptual Training in a Science Unit 141

LEARNING EXPERIENCES | EXPLANATORY NOTES

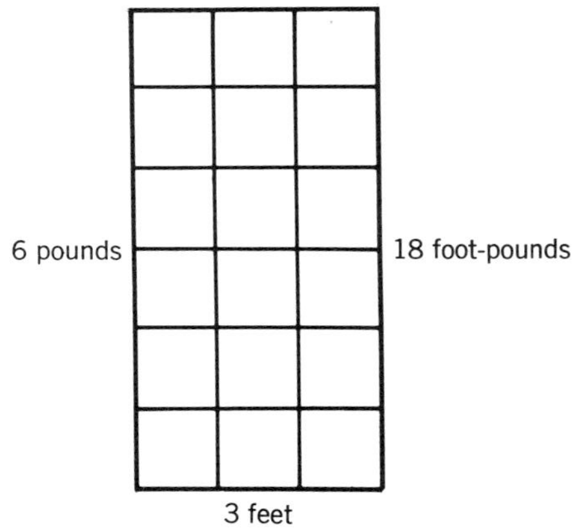

6 pounds | 18 foot-pounds | 3 feet

FIGURE 4-28. Using Energy Units with Small Forces

(10 pounds) and 1 inch wide (1 foot). Several of these strips should be divided into inches so that forces less than 10 pounds may be scaled. Use of those is shown in Figure 4-29.

142   *Perceptual Training in a Science Unit*

EXPLANATORY NOTES

Scaled strips placed underneath long strips

	10 pounds	10 pounds
	10 pounds	10 pounds
	10 pounds	10 pounds

66 foot-pounds

22 pounds

3 feet

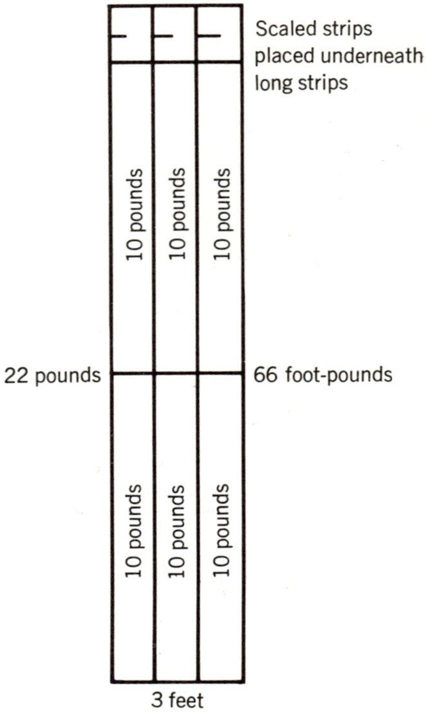

FIGURE 4-29. **Using Energy Units with Larger Forces**

LEARNING EXPERIENCES

LEARNING EXPERIENCES	EXPLANATORY NOTES
5.3 Have the children use the energy units to make energy rectangles for various combinations of actual energy expenditures; actually measuring the forces and distances as they slide bricks, slide one another, or perform the energy balance with the seesaw. Many other variations of using forces and distances will occur to the teacher. Include several instances where the same energy is developed with different combinations of force and distance, and have the children use the energy units to see how energy rectangles of different dimensions can have the same area. Counting the energy units in a given rectangle should conform to the teacher's preference for using these to aid in teaching multiplication. Vary by assigning hypothetical problems for the children to solve with the energy units.	

Basic Idea III: Power is the rate at which energy is produced or consumed.

LEARNING EXPERIENCES	EXPLANATORY NOTES
CONTENT A: *Power is a measure of how fast we exert energy.*	
4.1 Have the children measure various energy outputs and the number of seconds for each one. They can slide bricks, slide one another on the cloths, walk and run up a stair, and the like, each time measuring the force, the distance, and the time in seconds. For each such measurement the teacher should divide the energy by the number of seconds and announce the amount of power: "Let's see, Jim; you pulled 20 pounds 10 feet. That makes 200 foot-pounds. You did it in 5 seconds. That's 40 foot-pounds every second."	*Materials:* Stop watch, sturdy cloth for sliding children, stairway, bricks and strings for pulling, ropes, large and small spring scales. *General:* So far, the unit has dealt with energy as a quantity without regard to how fast or how slowly we produce it. In dealing with power, it is necessary to bring in the time element. Power is the amount of energy exerted (or consumed) in a unit of time. If a force of 50 pounds is exerted through a distance of 2 feet in 1 second, we can specify the amount of power simply by saying "100 foot-pounds per second."
4.2 Have each child perform one energy operation at two distinctly different rates; first slowly and then rapidly. Measure the energy and the time. Point out and discuss with the children that different amounts of power must be used to do the same amount of work when we change the *time.* They can experience this; that is, they must work "harder" to do a given task when they speed up their efforts.	*General:* One child can pull another on a cloth for 6 feet with a force of 30 pounds. If he does this slowly the first time, it might take 10 seconds. On his second try (pulling the same child the same distance) he might do the same task in 3 seconds. Power for the first try is 18 foot-pounds per second; for the latter, power is 60 foot-pounds per second.
5.1 Have the children make a number of new energy units to a new scale, using a different color paper or tagboard from that used previously. Let each unit repre-	*Materials:* Tagboard or heavy construction paper, rulers, straightedges, scissors.

Perceptual Training in a Science Unit

LEARNING EXPERIENCES

sent 10 foot-pounds, and make each square 5 inches on a side; labeling each square "10 foot-pounds." Four of these squares can then be arranged so that they make a larger square. This larger square will then represent 40 foot-pounds, the amount of energy per second in our *manpower unit*. (See Figure 4-30.) To use these new unit squares to determine power output, have a child make the usual measurements of force, distance, and time, for an activity involving energy output. Have him use the "old" energy units first to determine only the energy. At this point, he will have a number which represents the number of foot-pounds of energy. Round off this number to the *nearest 10 foot-pounds* (762 would round off to 760; 766 would round off to 770, and so on). Now have him count out enough "new" units to total the amount of energy in the rounded-off number. He would count out 76 "new" units if his rounded number was 760 (each "new" unit is 10 foot-pounds). He then picks up all the new units and sorts them into equal piles; the number of piles corresponds to the number of seconds of time. At this point, each pile represents the number of foot-pounds per second. He then takes the unit squares *from one pile only*, and makes as many large 40-foot-pound squares from these as possible; the number of these large squares is the *manpower* developed in the original activity. Have each child measure the data for several activities, and determine the amount of "manpower" as outlined above.

EXPLANATORY NOTES

General: The unit will present now a means of determining graphically the amount of power developed in an operation involving energy output. The most common unit by which power is measured is *horsepower*; 1 horsepower is 550 foot-pounds per second. This unit is awkward; it vexes engineers, and it is much too large for present purposes, since it would require dealing with small fractions. Let us, therefore, invent our own unit of power. We will call it the *manpower*, and we will define 1 *manpower* as *40 foot-pounds per second*. This unit is strictly arbitrary, and does not necessarily bear any relation to the power which a man can develop.

General: To illustrate with a concrete example, assume a 70-pound child runs up a 10-foot (vertical distance) stair in 5 seconds. He would first use the "old" units to determine that the energy expended was 700 foot-pounds. He would then count out 70 of the new units (each one is 10 foot-pounds) to represent the energy of 700 foot-pounds. Since the time is 5 seconds, he would sort the 70 units into five piles, each pile being made as nearly equal to the others as possible. The sorting can be done in the same manner as one deals from a deck of cards. In this case, there would be fourteen units in each pile. He would then know that he had developed 140 foot-pounds of energy per second. He can arrange the fourteen new units into as many large squares (each large square being made up of four unit squares) as possible; in this case he could make three large squares with two small unit squares left over. By counting, he could determine that he had developed 3½ "manpower," as illustrated in Figure 4-31.

146   *Perceptual Training in a Science Unit*

EXPLANATORY NOTES

10 foot-pounds	10 foot-pounds
10 foot-pounds	10 foot-pounds

5-inch square: 10 foot-pounds

40 foot-pounds

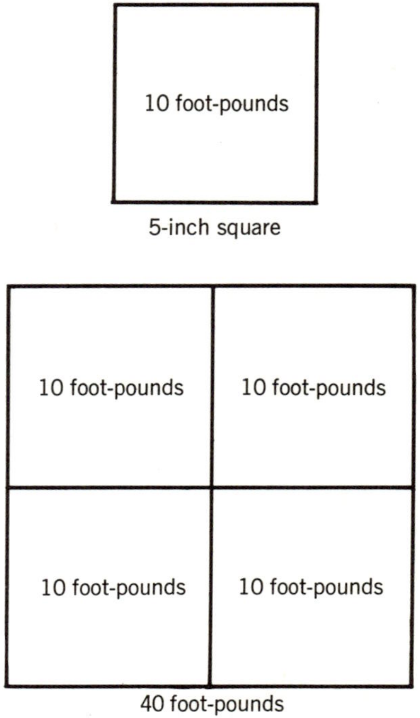

FIGURE 4-30. New Energy Units. One 5-inch square represents 10 foot-pounds.

LEARNING EXPERIENCES

Perceptual Training in a Science Unit   147

LEARNING EXPERIENCES	EXPLANATORY NOTES 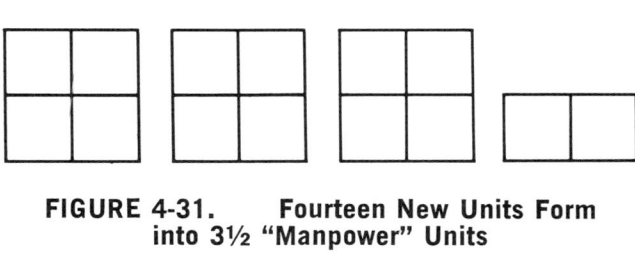
FIGURE 4-31. Fourteen New Units Form into 3½ "Manpower" Units
General: In sorting the units into piles, they will not, of course, always come out even. If the teacher wishes to avoid fractions, simply use a pile which is most typical. If the teacher wishes to deal with fractions, the extra units in some piles may be removed, cut up appropriately and distributed so as to equalize piles.

chapter 5

Perceptual Training in an Industrial Arts Unit

One general characteristic of the school program is the abstract, symbolic, and highly verbal nature of the academic process. This characteristic becomes more pronounced as the student advances to higher grade levels. More and more he is led away from manipulations of concrete objects, and is forced to deal with abstractions. Conceptualizing requires no overt involvement with the concrete. The academic process, therefore, offers progressively fewer occasions for promotion of developmental activities at the motor, motor-perceptual, and perceptual-motor levels.

Industrial arts studies and activities represent an exception to the foregoing observations. Most industrial arts training brings the student into active involvement with the concrete as opposed to the abstract. In planning perceptual training in conjunction with industrial arts, seldom does any need arise for introducing artificial or unusual activities. Abundant activities for perceptual training are present in the ongoing program. The teacher's task becomes one of utilizing opportunities which are naturally available — organizing, structuring, and highlighting certain aspects of the learner's experience to insure that the desired perceptual training arises from a given typical program.

CONDUCTING THE UNIT

Almost invariably, industrial arts subjects possess an inherent structure. Furthermore, the nature of the structure permits learning of that structure through direct involvement of a variety of sensory avenues. The structure may be experienced by the learner as he sees, hears, feels, and moves various elements in the learning situation itself. The goal of perceptual training in the industrial arts is to convey the inherent structure through the learner's various sense avenues in such a way that he is helped toward an inner structuring of himself as he interacts with concrete elements in the learning situation. Thus, a student who has some lack in his internal structure is brought into sensory-motor involvement with structured elements. The assumption behind this approach is that the slow learner's basic problem is some lack of inner structure, and that his basic learning problem can receive remediation through sensory-motor interaction with a structured situation.

Consider, for example, a student who experiences directional confusion. One simple activity to help remedy this basic problem is work with a socket wrench and ratchet handle in tightening and loosening bolts. Nearly all bolts and nuts have a "right-hand" thread; that is, in facing the bolt or nut a clockwise turning causes tightening and a counterclockwise turning causes loosening. When a student faces a bolt and attaches a socket wrench with ratchet handle, the handle becomes, in effect, the radius of a circle with the bolt at the center. The ratchet has two settings, one for tightening and the other for loosening. In tightening or loosening, the student receives visual, auditory, and tactual-kinesthetic feedback which is related to the direction of movement. The structure of the situation is such that each direction of turning provides its corresponding and distinctive feedback. When the student tightens a bolt he cannot avoid interacting with the inherent structure. His interaction produces feedback which in turn may be used to help him develop further his own internal structure.

Perceptual training will not come about automatically merely by arranging for the student to interact with a structured situation. The teacher must plan for developing activities which are generalized; without planning, the student will develop splinter skills instead of the internal structuring which he needs. In the preceding example, the student may come to approach all bolt-tightening tasks in a rigid way, using almost identical movements each time he engages in this activity. This practice is most undesirable. He needs, rather, to develop that flexibility which will let him bring to a given task a rich variety of generalized movement patterns from which he may draw as needed

Varying the movements by which any task is accomplished will increase flexibility and will help develop a more generalized internal structure. If the task is tightening a bolt with a socket wrench and ratchet handle, the student should be required to do this task from many different body positions. He should change hands occasionally. He should operate the ratchet handle from different positions relative to the location of the bolt; a movement of the handle at the "three o'clock" position, for example, requires an entirely different set of muscles than does the "nine o'clock" position. By introducing these and other variations, the structure of a bolt, with its built-in directional demands, provides an infinitely varied feedback to the student. The structure of the task does not change, but the student's interaction with the task changes greatly. True perceptual training arises from the student's internal organization of varied feedback from a given external structure.

The industrial arts teacher, therefore, has unique opportunities for combining perceptual training with the subject matter he is teaching. His task in this connection is not to devise activities for perceptual training. The activities are always close at hand in the form of the ongoing program. To provide perceptual training, the industrial arts teacher can analyze a particular task in terms of the student's interaction with that task—the sensory-motor avenues employed, the feedback which results, means of amplifying the feedback, and the possibilities for variation. From such an analysis should come new ways of involving the student so that the perceptual training is assured.

The unit of study in this chapter is presented as an illustration of how typical activities in industrial arts classes may be used for perceptual training. The unit title is: "Small Gasoline Engines: Disassembly, Assembly, Nomenclature, and Functioning." The assumed classroom situation involves a group of educable retarded teenagers in either a vocational training program or an industrial arts class in school. This group of students has been selected in order to illustrate maximum use of perceptual training in the unit. With only slight modifications by the teacher, the unit may be used with a regular class, emphasizing, in this case, the perceptual training aspects for those slow learners who need specific help.

The following materials and instructional aids for ten students and one instructor will be needed:

Two complete engines (air-cooled, one-cylinder, L-head, four-stroke cycle).

Two cylinder-block assemblies (engines, less head, carburetor, manifolds, tank, and other accessories).

Four hand cranks, approximately eight inches long and fabricated to replace engine drive pulleys or drive gears. These cranks are simple to construct, and will be used in turning engines by hand.

Four engine mounts, constructed of wood, to be used in mounting of engine to work bench. Use clamps to attach engine mount to bench. Construct mount so that engine may be clamped to bench in two different positions: piston vertical and piston horizontal.

One set of mechanic's tools, including socket wrench set (six-point sockets are preferred) with flex and ratchet handles.

One chalkboard.

One large wall chart showing the four strokes of the engine cycle. If a chart is not available, an appropriate filmstrip and projector may be substituted.

Two workbenches or tables.

The engines and the cylinder-block assemblies need not be in operating condition. If they are not immediately available, they may be purchased secondhand. In fact, items which are worn beyond normal use will be quite suitable for this unit. Engines and block assemblies in this condition are often discarded as junk by repair shops; often these discards will be given to the school without charge. It is recommended, however, that the two complete engines can be put in running condition without purchase of major parts. Putting two engines in running shape will provide a highly desirable success experience.

Each of the two work benches should have one complete engine and one cylinder-block assembly mounted on top and near one edge of the bench. Mount the engines with pistons vertical at first. The hand cranks should be attached so that when the piston is at top-dead-center the crank handle is at its highest point. A student should be able to turn the crank handle in a complete circle. Mount the engines and block assemblies so that two students can turn

Perceptual Training in an Industrial Arts Unit

cranks at the same time without mutual interference. The chalkboard should be visible from each work bench.

The unit is divided into three major sections:

    Section I: Functioning of the Engine
    Section II: Disassembly, Nomenclature, and Assembly
    Section III: Training in Sequencing and Sensory-Motor Integration

Unit activities are suggested under each section, with a parallel column noting concurrent perceptual training.

AN INDUSTRIAL ARTS UNIT:
SMALL GASOLINE ENGINES: DISASSEMBLY, ASSEMBLY, NOMENCLATURE, AND FUNCTIONING

Section I: Functioning of the Engine

ACTIVITIES	PERCEPTUAL TRAINING
1. Divide the class into two groups, one around each cylinder-block assembly. Explain that some parts have been removed to show how the main parts of the engine work together. Call attention to the complete engines and have students identify parts which are not on the block assemblies. Have students turn hand crank on block assembly, and point out that as the crank goes in a circle, the piston moves up and down. Have each one turn the crank while he uses his other hand to feel the simultaneous linear movement of the piston.	1. The major perceptual training at this stage is the tactual-kinesthetic experience of the interrelated and simultaneous rotary movement of the hand crank and the linear movement of the piston. Emphasize that when the engine is working, the piston makes the crankshaft turn, and that in turning the crank by hand the students are reversing the normal operation of the engine. Make clear that when the crank is at its topmost position, the piston is also at its topmost position. Let the students experience this operation by closing eyes, turning the crank, and feeling the piston move with other hand.
2. Use the block assembly to demonstrate the four strokes of the cycle: intake, compression, power and exhaust. Point out the interrelationships of parts for each of the strokes. The crank may be stopped at each stroke as the details are explained. Have each student feel the parts to further discover relative positions for each stroke. All explanations should be in terms of the dynamic functioning of the engine. For example, the intake valve is open on the intake stroke to let in the mixture of gasoline and air, while the downward motion of the piston causes this mixture to be drawn inward;	2. The emphasis should be upon synchrony. In the engine, as it operates, many events take place simultaneously and in relation to each other. The intake valve must open at the instant the piston is in a certain position, and so on. On most small engines, the size of parts will permit a student to place the heel of his palm on both valves, and at the same time keep several fingers of the same hand in contact with the top of the piston. His other hand can then be used to turn the crank. In this way he can feel the synchronous movements of major elements. This tactual-kinesthetic experience can be iso-

Perceptual Training in an Industrial Arts Unit 155

ACTIVITIES	PERCEPTUAL TRAINING
both valves are closed on compression and power strokes to seal in the mixture, and so on.	lated by having the student perform with eyes closed, adding the visual later when he has mastered the total experience tactually and kinesthetically. Let students feel the alternate vacuum and compression by placing palms over the cylinder while turning the crank.
3. Have each student demonstrate the four strokes beginning with the intake stroke, and explain all major events as he moves the crank from one position to another. At first the student should turn the crank to the intake stroke, stop, and then tell about the events that happen during the stroke; next, he should turn to the beginning of the compression stroke and describe the corresponding events, proceeding in this fashion through the entire cycle. When most of the group have mastered this activity, have everyone repeat the exercise, except this time the crank should be turned with a slow, continuous motion while the student describes appropriate simultaneous events. A typical description might begin, "The intake valve is open; the piston is moving down; the gas and air are coming in; now both valves are closed and the piston is coming up on the compression stroke; now the piston is at the top and the spark plug fires; the explosion is pushing the piston down. . . ."	3. Verbal activity is now being added to the total situation. Data from speech mechanisms and auditory feedback are added to visual and tactual-kinesthetic data. When all these data come together at once, some students may not be able to keep them organized. First, try to have such a student slow down the process. Then have him try to perform with eyes closed; incoming visual data may be causing confusion. If removing the visual data brings no improvement, the motor activity involving speech may be interfering with other body activities. This interference may be checked by having someone other than the student slowly describe the cycle aloud while the student tries to turn the crank to correspond with the verbal description. These procedures may help isolate the problem; use of the engine for remediation will be discussed in Section III of this unit.
4. Have each of the two groups gather around the complete engine. Remind them that everything which took place in the block assembly happens inside the complete engine, except that now they can see only the crank	4. This activity provides excellent training in perceptual-motor matching. The following data are arriving simultaneously for processing: a. Visual data obtained from visual monitoring of

ACTIVITIES

move. *Disconnect the spark plug wire to avoid accidental starting, and caution against touching the terminal.* Have students turn the crank on the complete engine, and see if some of them can feel movements and listen to sounds which will tell them where the piston is at a given moment. Point out that the position of the crank will tell them where the piston is, and that by listening carefully they can find out how the sound of the intake stroke differs from the sound of the exhaust stroke. Also, the crank will turn hardest when the piston is moving up on the compression stroke, and it will turn easiest when it is moving down on the power stroke. From these clues, they should be able to determine where the now invisible piston is at all times; knowing this, they should also be able to determine which valves are open or closed at all times. The teacher should help those who have difficulty, giving help mainly in the form of bringing more of the student's data-processing mechanisms into play. When the class is able to determine and to describe the internal activity in the complete engine, have them take turns describing what happens while turning the crank.

5. Remove the spark plug from each complete engine. Place a pencil through the hole left by the spark plug, and

PERCEPTUAL TRAINING

movements. The location of the crank is established partly from visual data as the student observes both the crank and his hand turning the crank.

b. Tactual-kinesthetic feedback from the muscular activity in turning the crank. These data help establish crank position, and provide the same information as is received through the visual channel. In addition, tactual-kinesthetic feedback is a clue for determining when the piston is moving up on compression (this stroke requires the most turning effort) or down on the power stroke (this stroke requires the least turning effort).

c. Auditory data from the sound of air rushing in during the intake stroke and rushing out during the exhaust stroke.

Students should be given ample opportunity to experience the simultaneous arrival of the three types of data. Insist that they watch the hand as they turn the crank. This activity should extend well beyond the point where the student is able to identify each stroke; he should overlearn. Provide generalization by clamping the motor to the bench in different positions: piston horizontal and pointing left, then right; piston down; crankshaft vertical with hand crank turning in a horizontal plane, first with crank on top, then with crank on bottom. Put motor on floor, and operate from varied positions.

5. These activities are for further generalization. Perceptual data are still received, but they come more indirectly

Perceptual Training in an Industrial Arts Unit 157

ACTIVITIES

let the end of the pencil touch the top of the piston. Have a student hold the pencil steady while turning the crank. Call attention to the up and down movement of the pencil, and emphasize that the piston is moving the pencil. Have students take turns cranking. Next, remove the pencil, and have a student turn the hand crank while all listen to the new and distinctive sound of compressed air rushing out of the spark plug hole during the compression stroke. Have the student distinguish the sounds peculiar to each stroke in this new situation. While spark plug is removed, connect ignition wire to spark plug and place plug on engine. Turn crank to let students see spark. Point out that the spark occurs at the top of the compression stroke. Let the student press a thumb over the spark plug hole and feel the force of compression as the piston comes up on the compression stroke. The student should be able to differentiate the compression stroke from all others by using only this clue. Have the student perform this last activity with ears plugged and eyes closed. Students should take turns on all activities.

PERCEPTUAL TRAINING

than in previous experiences. For example, the student still feels the movement of the piston, but only indirectly through the related movement of the pencil. He cannot see the piston move, but he can see the pencil which the piston causes to move. The same type of indirect experience arises from putting the thumb over the spark plug hole and feeling the pressure during the compression stroke.

For certain children, such activities, involving indirect perceptual experience of unseen objects and events, can be extremely important. It appears that for some children an object or event ceases to exist whenever the object or event is no longer visible. Such a child may look at an object and comprehend it as part of his world. When he turns his back on the object, however, that object seems to pass from his world. It is as if the object no longer exists for the child when he cannot see it. Piaget (Hunt, 1961, pp. 129-130)[1] notes that objects normally begin to acquire permanence for the infant from 4½ to 8 or 9 months; a search for an object which is removed from his vision will occur. Before this development, when the object vanishes from vision it does not elicit searching. Some older children with learning problems seem not to have developed a sense of object permanence when the object is not seen.

---

[1] J. McV. Hunt, *Intelligence and Experience.* Copyright© 1961. The Ronald Press Company, New York.

ACTIVITIES

PERCEPTUAL TRAINING

The teacher should be alert for students who show indications of this pattern of behavior. The following activities will provide extra help for these students:

a. Begin with the student operating the block assembly (the piston is visible). Have him turn the crank with one hand while fingers of the other hand remain in contact with the moving piston. See to it that he watches closely the hand on the piston, and looks occasionally at the hand on the crank. Have him describe only the movement of the piston while he turns the crank, saying something similar to this: "On top . . . going down . . . on bottom . . . coming up . . . on top . . . ." Have him do also with eyes closed.

b. When he has mastered this assignment, have him hold a pencil on top of the piston (that is, the piston in the block assembly) and turn the crank while watching the hand on the pencil, the pencil, and the piston. He describes the movement in the same fashion as before. Have him do also with eyes closed.

c. When the foregoing performance is satisfactory, tape a piece of paper over the cylinder of the block assembly so that the piston is no longer visible. Punch the pencil through the paper, and have him hold the pencil in contact with the piston while turning the crank. Again he watches hand and pencil movements while describing the movements aloud. Have him perform with eyes closed.

d. Now have him go to the complete engine, place the pencil through the spark plug hole so that the pencil

Perceptual Training in an Industrial Arts Unit

ACTIVITIES	PERCEPTUAL TRAINING
	touches the piston, hold the pencil against the piston while turning the crank, watch the hand and pencil, and describe at the same time the movement of the *piston*. Have him close his eyes, turn the crank, and tell where the piston is. Vary by having him stop on teacher's command, and then say where the piston is. e. Vary by having him hold the pencil while someone else turns crank; he tells where the piston is.
6. Show the wall chart to the class. The wall chart should consist of four schematic diagrams showing the four strokes of the cycle. Volunteers may explain each stroke, pointing to applicable portions of the chart as they speak. All should attempt the explanation from the chart. For those who have trouble, go back to the block assembly, then back again to the chart.	6. With the wall chart, the student moves a small step away from concrete experience and takes a small step toward a symbolic representation of the concrete. Note, however, that a foundation of concrete experience and perceptual organization of that experience was provided before the symbolic representation was added.
7. Position the chalkboard so that each student can see one of the block assemblies and can look at the chalkboard without changing his position unduly. Have one student operate each block assembly. The student operator sets the piston at the beginning of the intake stroke. Members of the class then describe everything which takes place during that stroke, and the teacher writes their descriptions on the board under the heading, "Intake Stroke." The procedure is repeated for each stroke, in order. Students then copy what is written on the board. After this activity, some students may be able to write	7. This activity is presented as only one example of connecting the symbolic activity of reading and writing to the perceptual activity associated with concrete experience. The teacher should add reading and writing to the unit activities whenever possible. For many children, little or no connection seems to exist between words on a page and concrete experience. Industrial arts subjects provide a unique opportunity to help the student make this important connection.

ACTIVITIES	PERCEPTUAL TRAINING
descriptions in their own words. Such assignments should be made at the teacher's discretion. 8. Explain the ignition and carburetion systems to the class.	8. In presenting the carburetion system, low pressure can be experienced by having the student place his palm over the cylinder while the piston is moving down. Show how the intake valve makes an opening between the cylinder and the carburetor. On the complete engine, let him feel the low pressure at the carburetor (air cleaner removed). In presenting the ignition system, the main relationship which can be perceived directly is the interrelatedness of the spark, the ignition points, and the ignition cam.

Section II: Disassembly, Nomenclature, and Assembly

ACTIVITIES	PERCEPTUAL TRAINING
1. Divide the class into four groups, each group to work with an engine or a block assembly. Each group should disassemble its engine or block assembly under supervision of the teacher. At appropriate stages of the disassembly, the teacher may point out relationships which could not be seen clearly while the engine was assembled. The most important of these is the relationship between the camshaft and the valves. Students should learn the correct names of the more important	1. Before disassembly begins, the teacher might explain the importance of direction in tightening the loosening bolts. Use socket wrenches and handles for student experience. Point out how a clockwise direction tightens a bolt only if the student faces the bolt; the direction reverses if the bolt faces away from the student. Students should also practice estimating the size socket needed for a particular bolt or nut, checking each estimate by trying to fit the wrench to the bolt or nut.

ACTIVITIES

parts, and they should learn to write them and to recognize the written names.

2. With the engine (or block assembly) disassembled, have students select parts which can be fitted together on the basis of form or patterns of holes. Have them pair off, with one student of a pair selecting a part for the other to match through clues from form or pattern. When a student thinks he has found a match, he should try it for fit.

3. Assembly of the engine and block assemblies should have detailed supervision from the teacher. Each group should select the parts which that group thinks should be assembled first. They should explain to the teacher what they plan to put together and point out exactly how they propose to do so. Then another logical group of parts is selected, and the process is repeated until the engine is complete. If the teacher notes that the students' plan will result in problems, he may tell them that they are making a mistake, but should let them discover the mistake, checking new plans with him before proceeding.

PERCEPTUAL TRAINING

2. The perceptual training here is obvious. The teacher should note, however, that matching of form or pattern in this instance involves the student with unfamiliar shapes and configurations, but that an involvement with the perceptual organization of the whole has preceded involvement with the parts.

3. Whereas disassembly helps the student perceive the parts which make up the whole, assembly helps him perceive the whole as coming together from the parts. In suggesting a detailed supervision pattern, the aim is to provide experience in dealing with the logical sequence in which elements must come together. For example, one group may want to put the cylinder head and crankshaft on before installing the piston and connecting rod. In most small engines, this order will not work. Usually, either the cylinder head or the crankshaft may be installed before installing the piston and connecting rod, but not both. Students should be exposed to this kind of problem in assembling the engine.

Each student should make at least one gasket for use on the engine. Making a gasket is excellent perceptual training. The method which offers maximum perceptual training is the one used frequently by mechanics: Gasket material is held firmly against the part surface, and a

162 Perceptual Training in an Industrial Arts Unit

ACTIVITIES	PERCEPTUAL TRAINING
	shop hammer is used to tap around the part outline. The tapping is concentrated at the edges, and forces the gasket material against the edge. The edge cuts through the gasket material, and when all edges have been tapped sufficiently the gasket is in proper form. Tapping out bolt-holes should be done with the rounded end of the hammer. This task requires the student to feel the outline of the part through the gasket material, and to use the feel to guide his tapping. Thus, the major sensory-motor avenues are involved.

Section III: Training in Sequencing and Sensory-Motor Integration

ACTIVITIES	PERCEPTUAL TRAINING
1. All activities in Section III use the two cylinder-block assemblies; complete engines will not be needed. Begin with piston vertical. With eyes closed, a student turns the crank with one hand. With the other hand he maintains continuous contact with valves and piston (heel of palm on valves and fingers touching piston). As he turns the crank, he describes what is happening, just as he did previously in Section I, 3. When he can perform this activity, the teacher has him stop, then move both hands clear of the engine, but keep eyes closed. The teacher then turns the crank several times, and stops the crank in any arbitrary position. The student explores the various parts	1. If the student has truly acquired a grasp of the sequence of events in the four cycles, he should be able to deal with isolated elements of the sequence. At any point in the sequence he should be able to relate that point to preceding and succeeding events, and to the sequence as a whole. With his eyes closed, he uses only the tactual-kinesthetic feedback from exploratory movements to gain information about relative locations of engine parts. He can discover the valve positions, and from the position of the crank he can determine whether the piston would be moving up or down. This information is all he needs to know to determine the stroke and activities related to this position. He should perform this activity

Perceptual Training in an Industrial Arts Unit 163

ACTIVITIES	PERCEPTUAL TRAINING
with his hands only, and tells which stroke is operating and what is happening in this position. He opens his eyes afterward to check his performance.	with the engine in various positions, and with his body in various relations to the engine.
2. Repeat the preceding activity, but with eyes open. The student turns his back to the engine while the teacher sets the crank in an arbitrary position. When the teacher has set the crank, the student looks at the engine. He is to explore it only with his eyes now. He then announces the stroke, and describes what is happening at this instant represented by the setting. Repeat activity with settings from all four strokes, varying not only the stroke, but also varying positions within a given stroke.	2. For most students, this activity should not be attempted until the student has mastered the one immediately above. However, if a student can perform with eyes open, but cannot do so when he closes his eyes, he may be helped by reversing the usual order. In this case, he should first describe the sequence while someone else turns the crank (thus eliminating all sensory channels except the visual); then he should turn the crank while watching and feeling all movement; finally he should close his eyes and perform as in III, 1. In the more typical situation, it is expected that the visual organization will follow the motor. Thus, this activity begins with the student who has mastered the motor organization, adding training in visual organization to the motor organization.
3. Have the students stand or sit facing the chalkboard. Place a block assembly behind the students, and place a screen between them and the block assembly. Write the name of one of the strokes on the board ("exhaust stroke," for example). Have a student go behind the screen and turn the crank to correspond with the stroke written on the board.	3. This activity requires the student to perform a sequence of activities. He must (1) read the name of the stroke, (2) remember what he has read while he walks to the block assembly, (3) solve the problem of the sequence of events within the engine, and (4) return to his place. Many children with learning problems cannot organize such a sequence of events in time; in dealing with one element, the others become lost or disorganized. The overt activity of walking to the block assembly will

ACTIVITIES	PERCEPTUAL TRAINING
	distract some to the point that they will not remember what they are to do when they arrive. This activity also helps connect written symbols with concrete experience.
4. Reverse the activity in 3 by setting the block assembly on a position; a student looks at the block assembly and writes the name of the stroke on the board. Vary by having the student explore the block assembly with eyes closed, and then write the name of the stroke on the board.	
5. Vary 3 by giving an oral command instead of writing the name of the stroke. ("Set the block assembly on the compression stroke.") Vary 4 by setting the block assembly on a certain position, and have the student announce the name of the stroke.	5. The teacher should be alert for the student whose performance of activities 3, 4, or 5 reveals marked differences. This clue may suggest that one or more sensory-motor avenues are functioning at a lower level than others. For example, if performance on activity 5 is much better than on 3, vision may be functioning at a lower level than audition. The teacher may modify activity with the block assembly to help isolate a particular sensory-motor avenue which is causing trouble. Activities 3, 4, and 5 require use of vision, audition, and motor activity. By selective modification of these activities, the teacher may remove first one and then another to determine relative functioning.

Appendix

Constructing a Styrofoam Sphere

The sphere is made from 1-inch thick sheets of styrofoam. The sheets are the type sold by building supply firms for home insulating purposes; this variety is a lower grade and much less expensive styrofoam than that sold for craft and hobby use.

The foundation of the sphere is formed by stacking progressively smaller styrofoam rings on top of each other until a rough hemisphere is built. The procedure is repeated for a second hemisphere, and the two are joined to make a rough sphere. The surface is completed by applying papier-maché clay to the outside, forming a smooth and continuous surface. See Figure A-1 for cross-section view of one hemisphere.

To cut rings from styrofoam sheets, the inner and outer diameters of each ring must be determined. The following procedure will give these diameters by direct measurement and without the necessity of making mathematical computations:

1. On a large sheet of paper draw full-scale a half-circle of the same radius you wish the finished sphere to have. Draw the diameter and one radius perpendicular to the diameter (Figure A-1).

2. Measure the thickness of one styrofoam sheet (it may not be exactly 1 inch). Beginning at the center of the half-circle, measure *along the radius* and make marks on the radius, dividing

Appendix

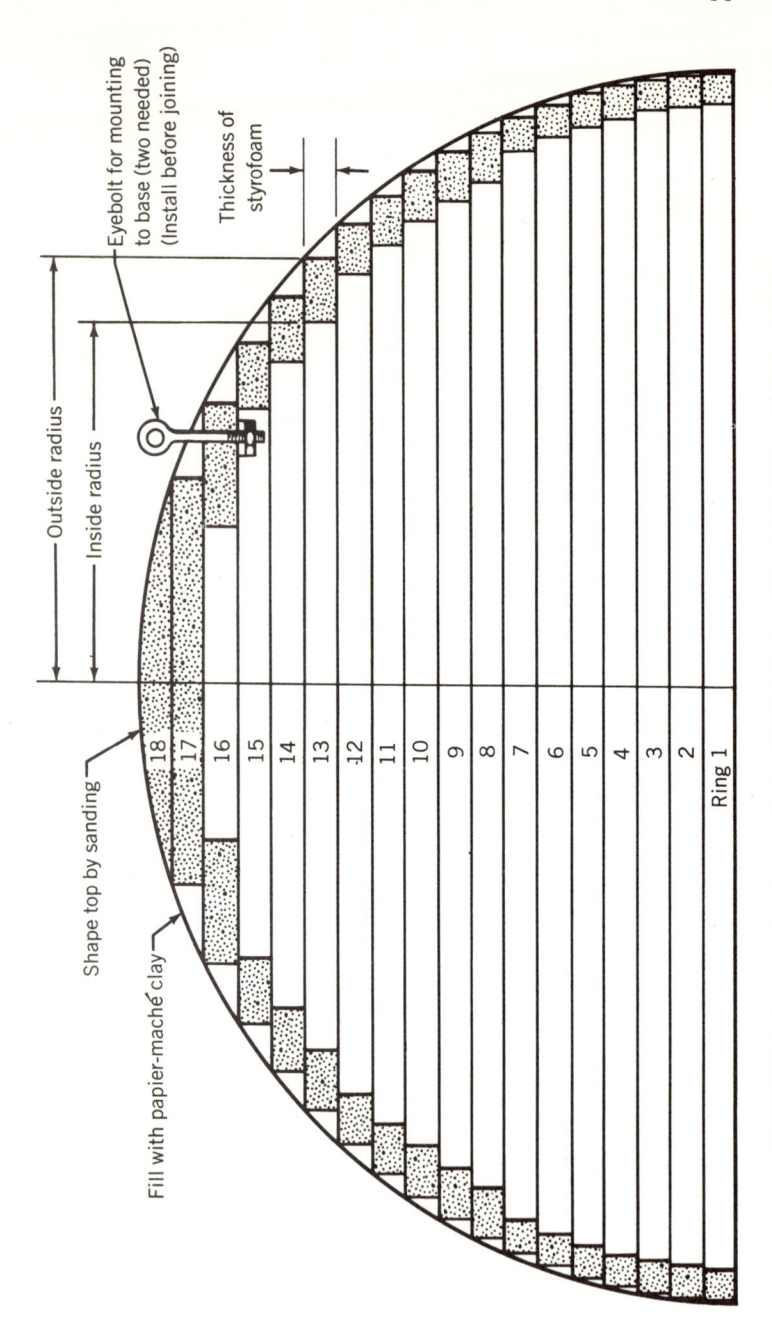

FIGURE A-1. Cross-section of Styrofoam Rings Forming Hollow Sphere

Appendix

the radius into short lengths equal to the thickness of one styrofoam sheet. Draw lines through these marks, making the lines parallel to the diameter line; each line should extend to the edge of the half-circle.

3. The outside radius of each ring can now be measured directly. Measure from the half-circle radius line to the edge of the half-circle, measuring along the parallel lines (Figure A-1).

4. The inside radius of each ring should be such that each ring will have adequate contact surface to join with and support the immediately adjacent smaller ring. Examine Figure A-1 carefully, and note that as outside diameters become smaller the widths of the rings must increase in order to make contact. If a 36-inch diameter sphere is being made, the following information will apply to inner radii of rings 1 inch thick (Figure A-1).

Rings 1 through 7: Make inside radius 1-inch smaller than outside radius.

Rings 8 through 12: Make inside radius 1½ inches smaller than outside radius.

Rings 13 through 15: Make inside radius 2 inches smaller than outside radius.

Ring 16: Make inside radius 4 inches smaller than outside radius.

Note: Cover (No. 17) and Top (No. 18) are solid.

5. When inside and outside radii for all rings have been determined, the rings may be marked out and cut from styrofoam sheets with a hacksaw blade. To start a cut, push one end of blade through the styrofoam sheet at a convenient starting point on the ring outline and begin sawing. Side of blade should be kept as nearly perpendicular as possible to the styrofoam sheet, so that sawed edges will not be slanted.

6. Glue rings together to form two hemispheres. Toothpicks may be pushed through rings to hold them while glue dries. *Important*: Use type glue recommended by your supplier, since some types react chemically with styrofoam. Let glue dry. Use rough sandpaper to form top into spherical shape (Figure A-1). Insert two eyebolts (with washers and nuts) into ring 16 of *one hemisphere* only, before joining hemispheres (Figure A-1). These eyelets are for anchoring to base.

7. Fill in the outer spaces with papier-maché clay, smoothing the clay into a uniform spherical surface.

8. When the clay has dried, use sandpaper to smooth and shape any rough or uneven areas. Paint with two coats of latex-base paint, using heavy sand-float finish with second coat.

9. A fairly large plastic laundry basket will make a good base. Place the globe on the basket with the eyebolts down (Figure A-2). Shift the globe so that the eyebolts are approximately the same distance from the sides of the basket. Tie stout cords from each eyebolt to the side of the basket, tying cord ends well below the eyebolts. Neither eyebolt should be in the location of the South Pole.

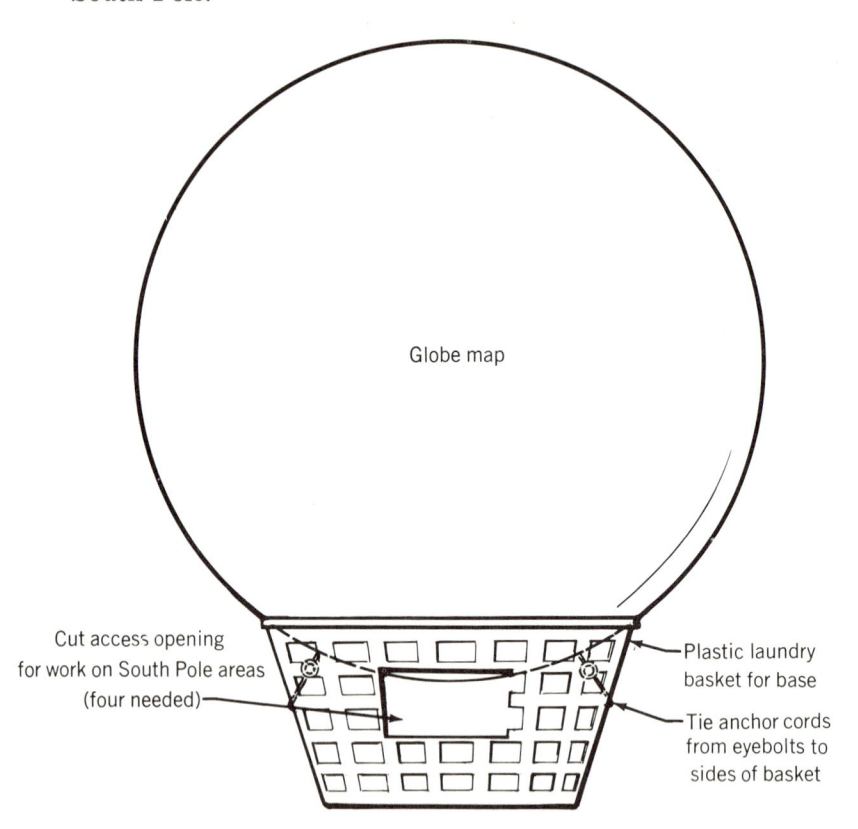

FIGURE A-2. Mounting the Globe Map on a Base

10. Cut four openings in the basket for future access to lower part of globe. Openings should be equally spaced, and should be large enough to permit inserting arms for drawing in South Pole areas.

Bibliography

Coghill, G. E., *Anatomy and the Problem of Behavior*, Cambridge: Cambridge University Press, 1929.

Dunsing, Jack D., and Newell C. Kephart, "Motor Generalizations in Space and Time" in *Learning Disorders*, ed. Jerome Hellmuth (Seattle, Washington: Special Child Publications, 1965), I, 77-121.

Durrell, Donald D., *Durrell Analysis of Reading Difficulty*, New York: Harcourt, Brace & World, Inc., 1955.

Frostig, Marianne, *Developmental Test of Visual Perception*, Palo Alto, California: Consulting Psychologists Press, 1963.

Hagin, Rosa A., Archie A. Silver, and Marilyn F. Hersh, "Specific Reading Disability: Teaching by Stimulation of Deficit Perceptual Areas," in *Reading and Inquiry*, ed. J. Allen Figurel, Newark, Delaware: International Reading Association, 1965, X, 368-70.

Harris, Albert J., *How to Increase Reading Ability* (4th ed., rev.), New York: David McKay Company, Inc., 1961.

Hunt., J. McV., *Intelligence and Experience*, New York: The Ronald Press Company, 1961.

Kephart, Newell C., *The Slow Learner in the Classroom*, Columbus, Ohio: Charles E. Merrill Books, Inc., 1960.

Kirk, Samuel A., *Teaching Reading to Slow-Learning Children*, New York: Houghton-Mifflin Company, 1940.

Roach, Eugene, and Newell C. Kephart, *The Purdue Perceptual-Motor Survey*, Columbus, Ohio: Charles E. Merrill Books, Inc., 1966

Rutherford, W. L. "Perceptual-Motor Training and Readiness," in *Reading and Inquiry*, ed. J. Allen Figurel, Newark, Del.: International Reading Association, 1965, X, 294-296.

Slingerland, Beth H., *Screening Tests for Identifying Children with Specific Language Disability*, Cambridge: Educators Publishing Service, 1964.

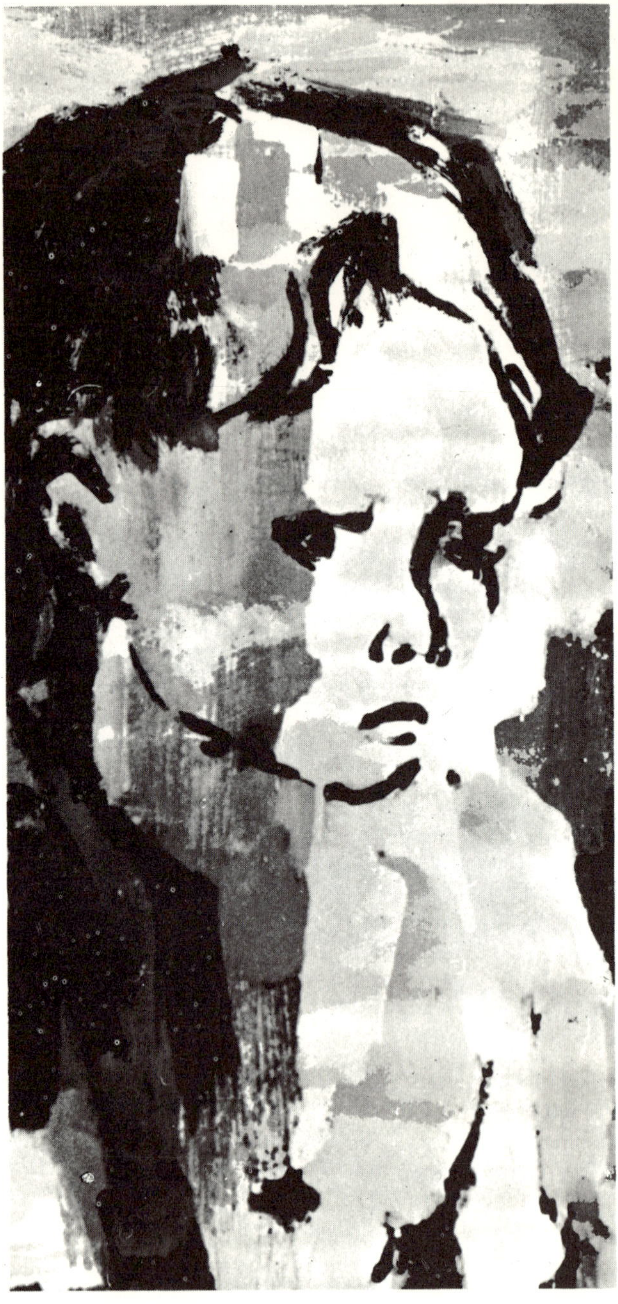

Index

Index

Auditory perception, 17-18 (*see also* Perceptual-motor match)

Coghill, G. E., 12
Concepts, 23
Coordination (*see* Integration)
Curriculum activities and perceptual training, 27-31 (*for specific training activities see also* Language arts curriculum unit, Science curriculum unit, Social studies project for perceptual training, *and* Vocational training curriculum unit)

Diagnosis of perceptual problems (*see* Evaluation of perceptual problems)
Differentiation of body parts, 12-13 (*see also the following listings under* Perceptual training: Perceptual-motor match, Balance and posture, *and* Body image and differentiation)
  direction and sequence of, 12
  educational implications, 12
Dunsing, Jack D., 7, 21
Durrell Analysis of Reading Difficulty, 25
Durrell, Donald D., 25

Environment
  relation to development of child, 9-10
  space, 15-20
  structure and organization of, 7
Evaluation of perceptual problems, 24-27, 64, 66-69, 71-73, 78-79, 83, 155, 157-158, 163-164
Eye-hand coordination, 19-20 (*see also* Perceptual-motor match)

Form perception (*see listing under* Perceptual training)
Frostig, Marianne, 24

Generalized movement patterns, 13-14 (*see also the following listings under* Perceptual training: Integration and generalization)
Gravity: its role in developing laterality, 16

Hagin, Rosa A., 26
Hand-eye coordination, 19 (*see also* Perceptual-motor match)
Harris, Albert J., 61-62
Hersh, Marilyn F., 26

Industrial arts curriculum unit, 149-163
  goals, 150-152
  training from curriculum activities:
    directionality, 150-151, 160
    form perception, 161-162
    generalization, 156-159
    perceptual-motor match, 154-159, 161-164
    sequence, 162-164
    synchrony, 154, 162-164
  unit outline, 153
Integration of body parts, 13 (see also Generalized movement patterns, and the following listings under Perceptual training: Integration and generalization)
Internal structure of the child, 7-10
  definition, 7-8
  development of internal structure, 11-15
  developed through interactions with environment, 9-10
  educational implications, 9
  motor basis of internal structure, 10-11
  related to structure of environment, 7

Kephart, Newell C., 7, 12, 21
Kinesthetic perception, 10-11, 17-18 (see also the following listings under Perceptual training: Perceptual-motor match, Form perception, Balance and posture, and Body image and differentiation)
Kirk, Samuel A., 61

Language arts curriculum unit, 61-90
  experience chart reading method, 61-62, 89-90
  goals, 62
  playing kickball as perceptual experience, 62-65
  training from curriculum activities:
    balance and posture, 77, 79-83, 85
    body image and differentiation, 77, 79-83, 85
    directionality, 68-70
    form perception, 68-70, 79-81, 86-87
    ocular control, 80, 87
    perceptual-motor match, 79-81, 85-87
    rhythm, 66-68
    sequence, 66-68
    spatial relations, 68-70, 71-72
    synchrony, 66-68
    temporal-spatial relations, 72
Laterality, 15-16 (see also the following listings under Perceptual training: Balance and posture, Body image and differentiation, and Perceptual-motor match)
  development, 16
Levels of perceptual development, 23, 93, 95-96

Marianne Frostig Developmental Test of Visual Perception, 24-25
Motor base, 11-15
  definition, 11
  relation to perceptual development, 18-20
Motor basis of internal structure, 10-11
Motor level of perceptual development, 23, 93-95
Motor organization (see Internal structure of the child)
Motor-perceptual level of perceptual development, 23, 93, 95

Index

Perceptual-conceptual level of perceptual development, 23, 93, 95-97
Perceptual Development
 levels of development, 23
 motor basis, 10-11
 theory of, 6-23
Perceptual level of perceptual development, 23, 93, 95-97
Perceptual levels of perceptual development, 23, 93, 95
Perceptual-motor level of perceptual development, 23, 93, 95
Perceptual-motor match, 17 (see also Perceptual training for training activities)
Perceptual Problems, 3-4 (see also Evaluation of perceptual problems)
Perceptual training
 curriculum as a source, 27-31
 general considerations, 23-27
 in curricula, 4-5
 related to academic achievement, 26-27
 training from curriculum activities:
  balance and posture, 77, 79-83, 85
  body image and differentiation, 36-37, 77, 79-83, 85
  differentiation, 98-99, 102, 106-109
  directionality, 36, 101-103, 111, 150-151, 160
  form perception, 36-38, 68-70, 79-81, 86-87, 103-105, 111-132, 161-162
  integration and generalization, 36-38, 98-101, 103-109, 121-122, 156-159
  ocular control, 80, 87
  perceptual-motor match, 36-38, 79-81, 85-87, 99-107, 110-112, 154-159, 161-164
  rhythm, 66-68
  sequence, 66-68, 162-164
  spatial relations, 36-38, 71-72
  synchrony, 66-68, 98-100, 102-104, 154, 162-164
  temporal-spatial relations, 39, 72
Purdue Perceptual-Motor Survey, 24-25

Remediation of learning disabilities (see also Perceptual training)
 curriculum as a source of remediation, 27-31
 general, 23-27
Rhythm, 21-22 (see also under Perceptual training)

Science curriculum unit, 93-147
 energy, 95-96, 132-143
 force, 93-95, 98-131
 goals, 93
 power, 144-147
 training from curriculum activities:
  differentiation, 98-99, 102, 106-109
  directionality, 101-103, 111
  form perception, 103-105, 111-132
  integration and generalization, 98-101, 103-109, 121-122
  perceptual-motor match, 99-107, 110-112
  synchrony, 98-100, 102-104
Screening Tests for Identifying Children with Specific Language Disability (Slingerland), 25
Sequence, 21-22 (see also under Perceptual training)
Silver, Archie A., 26
Slingerland, Beth H., 25

Social studies project for perceptual training, 33-59
  goals, 34-35
  perceptual training from project, 36-39
    differentiation, 36-37
    directionality, 36
    form perception, 36-38
    integration and generalization, 36-38
    perceptual-motor match, 36-38
    spatial relations, 36-38
    temporal-spatial relations, 39
  project materials, 39-59
    construction, 39-54
    use, 54-59
  project outline, 35-39

Spatial relations, 15-18 (*see also under* Perceptual training *and* Form perception)

Space, 15-20
  relation to internal structure of child, 16-17
Splinter skills, 12-13
Structure, internal (*see* Internal structure of the child)
Synchrony, 21-22 (*see also under* Perceptual training)

Time, 20-23
  relationship to motor development, 22
  relationship to space, 20-23
  temporal aspects of perception, 20-21

Verticality, 16
Vision, 16-20 (*see also the following listings under* Perceptual training: Ocular control *and* Perceptual-motor match)
  visual organization, 16-19